MODELLING AUDITORY PROCESSING AND ORGANISATION

Distinguished Dissertations in Computer Science

Edited by
C.J. van Rijsbergen, University of Glasgow

The Conference of Professors of Computer Science (CPCS) in conjunction
with the British Computer Society (BCS), selects annually for publication up
to four of the best British Ph.D. dissertations in computer science. The scheme
began in 1990. Its aim is to make more visible the significant contribution
made by Britain - in particular by students - to computer science, and to
provide a model for future students. Dissertations are selected on behalf of
CPCS by a panel whose members are:

M. Clint, Queen's University, Belfast
R.J.M. Hughes, University of Glasgow
R. Milner, University of Edinburgh (Chairman)
K. Moody, University of Cambridge
M.S. Paterson, University of Warwick
S. Shrivastava, University of Newcastle upon Tyne
A. Sloman, University of Birmingham
F. Sumner, University of Manchester

MODELLING AUDITORY PROCESSING AND ORGANISATION

Martin Cooke
University of Sheffield

CAMBRIDGE
UNIVERSITY PRESS

PUBLISHED BY THE PRESS SYNDICATE OF THE UNIVERSITY OF CAMBRIDGE
The Pitt Building, Trumpington Street, Cambridge, United Kingdom

CAMBRIDGE UNIVERSITY PRESS
The Edinburgh Building, Cambridge CB2 2RU, UK
40 West 20th Street, New York NY 10011–4211, USA
477 Williamstown Road, Port Melbourne, VIC 3207, Australia
Ruiz de Alarcón 13, 28014 Madrid, Spain
Dock House, The Waterfront, Cape Town 8001, South Africa

http://www.cambridge.org

First published 1993
First paperback edition 2005

A catalogue record for this book is available from the British Library

ISBN 0 521 45094 2 hardback
ISBN 0 521 61938 6 paperback

for Jo, Sam and Anna

Contents

Acknowledgments

It is a pleasure to thank all those individuals whose research has been influential in shaping this work. The strong auditory community of the UK is sufficiently cohesive to provide great help to anyone setting out on a modelling study such as the one described here. I have enjoyed productive discussions with research groups at the Universities of Cambridge (Roy Patterson and John Holdsworth), Edinburgh (Mark Terry), Keele (Bill Ainsworth and Ted Evans), Kiel (Michel Scheffers), Loughborough (Ray Meddis and Michael Hewitt), Nottingham (Quentin Summerfield and Richard Stubbs), Southampton (Bob Damper) and Sussex (Chris Darwin, Valter Ciocca and Roy Gardner), and with Roger Moore of the Speech Research Unit, RSRE.

I found collaboration with members of the Laboratoire D'Informatique pour la Mecanique et les Sciences de l'Ingenieur in Paris (Christophe D'Alessandro, Jean-Sylvain Lienard and Maxine Eskenazi) in the 1989 Cochleagram-Reading Workshop stimulating; in particular, the use of resynthesis was prompted by the work of Jean-Sylvain Lienard.

My interest in auditory modelling was inspired by David Schofield, a colleague of earlier days at the National Physical Laboratory, whose work in matching physiological and psychophysical accounts of frequency selectivity has, I believe, proved catalytic for later developments of the gammatone filterbank.

Thanks to: Steve Beet and Robin Sharpe for providing a good deal more insight into filter design and signal processing than I could have obtained from textbooks alone; Chris Darwin for the /ru/-/li/ stimulus used to illustrate grouping in Chapter 5; to the Centre for Speech Technology Research at Edinburgh University and the Department of Linguistics and Phonetics at Leeds for some of the utterances used; and to Lori Lamel for the loan of TIMIT.

Locally, I have enjoyed working with members of SPLASH, the SPeech LAboratory at SHeffield; particular credit must go to Malcolm 'disc-crasher' Crawford, who, apart from many stimulating discussions and all things confectionery, forced me to hit the return key on many crucial processes, when I preferred to pause contemplatively for a few minutes before discovering that an idea was not going to work. Thanks also to Guy Brown for proof-reading beyond the call and useful suggestions. Other members of the Department of Computer Science have, with a mixture of ribaldry and good-humour, made Sheffield a great place to work.

Special thanks are due to my supervisor, Phil Green, who had this work in mind from as long ago as 1984. His encouragement and confidence helped tremendously throughout.

The material presented in chapter 3 is re-expressed from a paper published in the journal Computer Speech and Language and is used with permission from Academic Press Ltd.

1

Introduction

1.1 Segregation and fusion in hearing

It has long been known that the auditory system decomposes signals reaching the ears at a very early stage of analysis, yet on listening to complex signals such as speech, we are primarily aware of wholes rather than parts. At some point, it must be necessary for the auditory system to re-integrate the component parts of the signal into structures which can be interpreted. If the auditory system could be sure that the incoming signal contained a single acoustic source, re-integration would be trivial (indeed, this model underlies most existing speech recognition devices). Problems arise when this approach is followed for signals which contain a mixture of acoustic sources, since any wholesale fusion of components would certainly confuse recognition systems expecting single sources.

A more sophisticated strategy, which the auditory system might adopt, is to determine which of the decomposed elements are likely to have arisen from the same acoustic source. In other words, it is possible to cast the main rôle of early audition as a search for meaningful organisation in analyses of the signal.

This thesis contains an account of a model which addresses precisely this question: What computational processes are required to make explicit organisation in auditory representations? The theoretical foundations for the model come from *auditory scene analysis* - a recent coherent account (Bregman [17]) of the factors and strategies which the auditory system appears to exploit in solving this problem.

Section 1.2 of this introductory chapter traces the evolution of speech and vision research, paving the way for a consideration, in section 1.3, of the wider theoretical influences which this work draws upon, leading to a discussion of auditory scene analysis in section 1.4. Previous approaches to the specific problems of segregating acoustic sources are reviewed in section 1.5.

1.2 Signals and symbols in machine perception

Before attempting to determine organisation in signals, it is necessary to consider the representational substrate upon which the search is to take place. We are immediately faced with what has become known as the 'signal-to-symbol' transformation (Green et al. [79]): how do we bridge the gap between continuous physical signals and discrete, symbolic descriptions of objects, whether auditory or visual?

Historically, researchers in computational vision have placed greater emphasis on a *representational* approach to machine perception than has been the case for speech. By contrast, work in automatic speech recognition (ASR) has largely been performance-driven, with scant attention paid to explanatory capabilities in models. Early approaches to machine vision and speech followed a roughly parallel course. Both fields were initially dominated by the Gibsonian view of perception as mediated by a collection of processes operating solely and directly on the raw stimulus (Gibson [71]). Such early attempts to partition speech or images directly into objects or words met with little success. Witkin and Tenenbaum [184] described the failure of attempts to find objects in images as the inevitable result of a task which "turned out to be prohibitively difficult, because it sought to bridge in a single leap the enormous gulf separating primitive image properties and high-level semantic descriptions". As a consequence, attention switched in the early 1970's to systems capable of accommodating top-down behaviour - the use of prior knowledge or expectations in image or speech interpretation (e.g. the Hearsay-II Speech Understanding System, Erman et al. [56]). From the late 1970's to the present, mainstream speech and vision research have diverged significantly. Speech research has employed a succession of machine-learning techniques, starting with template-matching (learning by rote), hidden Markov modelling (learning by observation) and latterly using connectionist models (learning by parameter adjustment). These approaches have in common the property that they are unable to formulate explanations, leading Fant [59], in his keynote address summarising the state of speech research, to the conclusion "We leave it to the computer to learn what we have failed to understand."

In contrast, work in machine vision has been heavily influenced by David Marr's computational theory of vision [117][118] since the mid-1970's. The insight, missing from earlier approaches, was that it is necessary to fully appreciate the computational problem posed by vision. Marr proposed a modular, functional description of problems in vision, observing that it was necessary to make explicit both the input required by a particular computation, and the representation computed. Marr, like Gibson, believed that much could be gained by data-driven processing; however, computations would not necessarily take place directly on the raw image; rather, Marr viewed vision as a series of representational transforms, each of which makes explicit some aspect of the preceding representation. Marr's approach has its roots in the Gestalt approach to perception (e.g. Wertheimer [179]), which states that objects are perceived as wholes, made by configurations of elements. The Gestalt psychologists described informally the rules which they believed gave rise to 'good' configurations. In Marr's computational theory, these rules become explicit constraints which facilitate an interpretation of the image and representations derived from it. Further consideration of Marr's work and its influence on speech and hearing research is provided in section 1.3.

Why is automatic speech recognition research not dominated by a similar approach? One possibility is that the full problem of vision confronted researchers early on - it is perhaps more difficult to find applications of computer vision in which the full vision problem can be avoided. In contrast, speech recognition research has developed in a sheltered acoustic environment quite unlike that faced by the auditory system. As a consequence of this emphasis on speech (which is, after all, only one type of acoustic source) rather than *hearing*, few mainstream speech researchers appreciate that the strategies adopted by the auditory system are unlikely to be similar to those used in ASR. Indeed, as late as 1987, Darwin and Gardner [42] still had good cause to write:

> The challenge to hearing from Marr's work is to understand sufficiently the
> computational problem posed by hearing. Only then will we be able to identify

what representations of the acoustic signal we need, and what constraints could mediate between them. (p. 113)

More recently, something approaching a computational theory of the function of early hearing has developed, largely due to the efforts of experimental psychologists studying sound source segregation. This body of work is reviewed in the next section.

1.3 Theoretical influences

Marr

Marr identified three levels at which work in computer vision should be understood, namely, *function*, *process* and *mechanism*. He argued that the function of a visual module must be clearly understood, independent of the process or algorithm devised to perform the function, which in turn should be kept separate from the implementation or mechanism of its solution. Interestingly, these are precisely the notions which are current in software engineering, where a clear separation between a functional specification of some task and its design and implementation is encouraged.

Software engineering employs abstractions of data in order to avoid unnecessary detail in the early stages of software construction. Marr made a similar point when he suggested that, as a consequence of a functional description of a vision module, it is necessary to make explicit the representational abstraction on which the module operates, and to state what is computed by that module. Specifically, he proposed that "the first step of consequence is to compute a primitive but rich description of the grey-level changes present in an image" (which Marr called the *primal sketch*). Later steps apply progressively higher-level constraints in order to make further levels of structure explicit.

Marr suggested a number of principles for the organisation of complex symbolic processes. The *principle of explicit naming* states that when a collection of data is to be described as a whole, it should be given a name and properties of it, as opposed to its parts, should be computed. The *principle of least commitment* states that, as far as possible, one should never do anything that may later have to be undone. The *principle of modular design* suggests that any computation should be split up and implemented as a collection of sub-parts which are as independent of each other as possible. Finally, the *principle of graceful degradation* aims to promote systems which are robust rather than brittle in the presence of data degradations.

Marrian influences in speech and hearing

Some computer scientists and experimental psychologists have argued for an adoption of Marr's basic philosophy in ASR and have cited the four principles outlined above when explaining auditory processes or as the motivation for algorithms (Darwin, Pattison and Gardner [43], p.341; Riley [142], p.89; Green et al. [79], p.186).

In 1981, Green and Grace [76] proposed a representational approach to acoustic-phonetics:

It has become a tenet of artificial intelligence research that to understand something one must first be able to adequately describe it. This approach has, for instance, been used to great effect in computer vision work by Marr. (p. 261)

An implementation of this proposal - coined the 'Speech Sketch' after Marr - was reported in Green and Wood [78]. Early versions of the Speech Sketch attempted to make explicit the temporal evolution of formant estimates (derived by LPC analysis) in order to support acoustic-phonetic reasoning. The system was applied to a semivowel recognition task; recognition was performed by matching frame-based representations of typical semivowel behaviour to descriptors in the Speech Sketch. Later work by Green and his colleagues [79] investigated alternative approaches to Speech Sketch construction and involved recasting the system into an object-oriented knowledge representation. Although this work was not directly motivated by models of auditory processing, Green and Wood [77] recognised that such an approach would be valuable:

> The grouping algorithms could, for instance, be applied to primitives closer to those which seem to be used in human speech perception, as suggested by Darwin [36]. (p. 338)

Darwin [38] was an early advocate of an auditory equivalent to Marr's primal sketch:

> ... it is a mistake to allow raw spectral information from the sound wave, or even properties extracted directly from the sound wave, to make immediate contact with stored knowledge on the properties of phonetic categories ... the lower level of auditory analysis should capture, for example, information about spectral peaks, local direction of movement in amplitude and frequency of energy regions, time of onset of energy in different regions, and so on. Such a description should then serve as a rich database for the operation of processes that can identify appropriate, more abstract structures. (p. 1646)

Several researchers attempted an analysis of speech spectrograms using operators suggested by Marr and others in computer vision (Leung and Zue [105]; Darwin and Stone [41]; Cooke and Green [28]), although it was recognised that simulating the performance of the human spectrogram reader was some way from modelling the function of hearing.

Work by Riley [142] on time-frequency representations is cast in a representational vein. Riley's goal was to form a rich description of a spectrogram - he called the process 'schematising spectrograms'. He argued for a representation in terms of the speech signal's physical origin, containing, amongst other things, descriptions which correspond to time-varying resonances, voice onsets and closures. His two-step model was influenced by Marr's representational transformations. The first step delivers a variety of 'reliable' features of the speech signal. The second step consists of a 'reconciliation' of these features with specific constraints (such as continuity of formants) about speech. Others have applied similar constraints to non-auditory representations (Cooke [29]; Laprie et al. [102]).

Seneff [158] attempted to create an explicit representation of the speech signal for use in a vowel recognition task. Starting from peaks in the auditory-based 'synchrony spectrogram', her model computes an orientation value for a proposed formant track passing through that peak. This results in a set of short line-segments, which are then subjected to an aggregation process. The resulting representation - the 'Skeleton Spectrogram' - is highly reminiscent of early versions of Green and Wood's 'Speech Sketch' [77].

Lienard [109] has developed a speech analysis technique which leads to an intermediate signal representation in terms of 'elementary waveforms', each defined by a small number of parameters. Elementary waveforms can be grouped according to similarity criteria. Lienard outlined a process for "tentative grouping of adjacent channels" but admits that the difficulty is in "determining which channels are to be grouped, and for how long". (p. 951).

1.4 Auditory scene analysis

Whilst the modelling approaches described above were, to a greater or lesser extent, influenced by ideas from the representational school of computer vision, they all lacked the insights that a clear statement of the computational problem facing hearing would bring. When such a statement was finally formulated, it came not from the modelling community, but from experimental psychology where researchers had appreciated these problems for some time. Although several researchers were instrumental in its development, the theoretical position is most coherently expressed in Bregman's book [17], whose title - *Auditory scene analysis* - is a compelling metaphor for the rôle of early auditory analysis.

Bregman summarises the task thus

> A central problem faced by audition was in dealing with mixtures of sounds. The sensory components that arise from distinct environmental events have to be segregated into separate perceptual representations. These representations (which I call streams) provide centers of description that connect sensory features so that the right combinations can serve as the basis for recognising the environmental events. (p.44)

Bregman's account details substantial experimental support for the notion that the auditory system exploits the organisation inherent in most complex signals. As an example, a set of sound components which are harmonically related (i.e. integer multiples of some common fundamental) are likely to be perceived as a coherent whole rather than as individual tones. Other principles which seem to bind components together perceptually include onset or offset synchrony, a common rate of amplitude modulation and frequency proximity, together with cues which suggest a common spatial origin. Some of these principles form part of the model of auditory perceptual organisation described in this thesis.

Although there is a difference in background and emphasis between the work of Marr and Bregman, it may be that Bregman's book will have an effect on computational work in speech and hearing similar to that which Marr's account had on vision. There are a number of high-level similarities between the two accounts (see also the discussion in Williams et al. [182]).

First, the two theories go a long way beyond a theoretical account; Marr addresses computational questions in depth, whilst Bregman brings together a wealth of experimental evidence in support of a scene analysis explanation of early audition. Next, both theories were influenced by the Gestalt psychologists, but Marr and Bregman answer the rightful criticism that the Gestaltists never expressed the laws of perceptual organisation in a concrete way. They stress the importance of functional descriptions in vision and audition by asking what perceptual organisation is for. Third, both favour a problem-solving approach, where heuristics actively compete to find explanations of the evidence. Finally, although the influence of top-down processes is acknowledged, both accounts mainly address primitive, bottom-up grouping processes.

The analogy between vision and hearing becomes strained as the more detail is added to the theoretical framework (see discussion in Bregman, chapter 1). However, although there is no direct equivalent in hearing to the recovery of 3D descriptions from a 2D projection, there are common problems in the two fields, particularly in finding correspondences. The stereo correspondence problem in vision - determining which parts of the image seen by the left eye match those parts seen by the right eye - has a direct analogue in the binaural correspondence problem. Similarly, the visual motion correspondence task - matching features in images taken at different times - is closely related to tasks such as tracking formants and harmonics.

1.5 Previous approaches to sound source segregation

There have been few computational attempts to seek organisation in an arbitrary mixture of acoustic sources, although several systems for separating the speech of two talkers have been described (Parsons [131]; Weintraub [176]). Most of the work on speech separation has attempted to model *simultaneous* segregation of double vowels within a single time frame, for which data on human performance is available. Some of this work is reviewed below. Systems which aim to go beyond static segregation meet a number of further problems in seeking *sequential* integration of components. For example, it is necessary to estimate the number of sources present at any time. However, a larger number of constraints become available for grouping algorithms, especially those derived from continuity of formants and harmonics. Weintraub's system was the first system which implemented both simultaneous and sequential organising principles with any sophistication, and is reviewed later in this section.

Double vowel separation

Scheffers [150] investigated the rôle that differences in the fundamental frequency of 2 simultaneous voiced sounds play in helping listeners to separate the pair. His main finding was that identification performance improved as the difference in F0 increased, asymptoting at around 1-2 semitones. He suggested that listeners might make use of spectral shape to identify at least one vowel in the pair, and tested this hypothesis by repeating the experiment with unvoiced vowels. Performance decreased, but was still at a level above chance, suggesting a contribution from both differences in F0 and spectral shape.

Several attempts to model the increase in vowel identification performance with increasing F0 difference have been made. Scheffers himself developed a two stage model of segregation which first estimated the two best fitting fundamentals using peaks in a simulated auditory excitation pattern, then sampled the excitation pattern at integer multiples of each F0 to generate a pair of 'separated spectra'. These spectra were further processed by a formant classifier which operated on peaks in the separated spectra. Scheffers found that the model performed rather less well than listeners, and, more importantly, did not show the same pattern of improvement with increases in F0 difference.

More recently, Assman and Summerfield [8] used autocorrelograms (ACGs) as a basis for double vowel segregation. An ACG is a representation of the fine temporal structure in a filterbank computed by autocorrelating the output of each filter (or some later transformation of the output) over a short time interval. The ACG is a powerful basis for pitch analysis since it responds to both resolved and unresolved components in the signal. Resolved harmonics of a periodic sound will produce peaks in the autocorrelation function at delays corresponding to the harmonic frequency and integer sub-multiples of it, including the fundamental. Unresolved harmonics can produce amplitude-modulation at a rate corresponding to their frequency difference, which again shows up in the autocorrelation function as a peak at this frequency. The potential of ACGs for sound source segregation has been noted by a number of researchers (Slaney and Lyon [165]; Duda, Lyon and Slaney [53]; Meddis and Hewitt [122]; Summerfield, Lea and Marshall [170]). Specifically, summing the ACG across channels as a function of autocorrelation delay enhances any common periodicity across channels.

Assman and Summerfield's strategy was to identify the two largest peaks in the compound ACG. They then computed the degree of synchrony to each of the 2 periods across the range of frequency channels. This procedure results in a pair of spectra, one for each periodicity. Vowels were then classified using a metric described elsewhere (Assman and Summerfield [7]). In addition to the 'place-time' autocorrelation model, Assman and Summerfield implemented a 'place' model similar to that of Scheffers described above, and further augmented the comparison with nonlinear versions of the two models. They compared the vowel identification performance of the four models with that of listeners, and found that the nonlinear place-time model came very close to predicting subjects results. An alternative separation mechanism is described in Summerfield, Lea and Marshall [170], together with a discussion of Meddis and Hewitt's approach.

Weintraub's system

The most extensive system for speech separation to date is that developed by Weintraub [176]. His final system consists of three main algorithmic components. In the first, a pitch-tracking algorithm determines the pitch period for each of two sources. The second module determines the number of sounds present and indicates whether each source is periodic or not. The third algorithm estimates the amplitude spectrum of each source.

The first stage uses a representation called a *coincidence function* operating on each channel of an auditory filterbank. The coincidence function is roughly comparable with the ACG described above, although there are some technical differences. His system averages a smoothed version of the coincidence representation across channels, producing an effect similar to that of a pooled ACG. An iterative dynamic programming algorithm then traces the stronger peak in the average coincidence function through time. This process is repeated for a peak corresponding to a weaker pitch.

Estimating the number of sources and their periodicity/nonperiodicity was accomplished using a 7-state Markov model for each sound source. The states were decided upon *a priori*, whilst transition probabilities came from hand-labelled training data. In the model, a sound source could be silent, periodic, nonperiodic, or be in one of four transitional states: onset, offset, increasing periodicity or decreasing periodicity. Without detailed justification, Weintraub imposed the artificial constraint that only one sound source could be in a transitional state at any time.

Weintraub's spectral estimation algorithm uses information about the state each source is in to decide how to split the energy in each frequency region. The algorithm uses pre-stored histograms of amplitude ratios obtained from a training database to generate an initial estimate of the spectral amplitude of each source, then iteratively applies local spectral continuity constraints to determine smoothly-varying amplitude contours.

The system was evaluated in part by feeding waveforms resynthesised from separated spectra into a recognition system (other evaluation mechanisms used in his system are reviewed in chapter 6 of this thesis). The resultant recognition rates were compared with those obtained by simply feeding the mixed (non-segregated) waveform into the recogniser. His results are somewhat inconclusive and difficult to interpret. For example, the system improved the ability of the recogniser for a male voice, but degraded that for a female.

Discussion

Computational approaches to sound source segregation are few in number, reflecting how recently this problem has been recognised as a fundamental task of early hearing. The selection of work presented above was restricted to those methods which employed auditory models. There have been several non-auditory attempts to solve aspects of this problem (Parsons [131]; Moore et al. [128]; Zhao and Denbigh [188]). The approach of Moore et al. is interesting because it makes no attempt to segregate the mixture using primitive, bottom-up processes, but uses the best explanation in terms of two simultaneous hidden Markov model sequences. In contrast to virtually all other modelling accounts of source segregation which use pitch as the sole cue, Zhao and Denbigh's system [188] attempts to determine onsets of new sources.

Perhaps the main limitations of previous approaches stem from their emphasis on *speech* source separation and the way in which time is handled. Whilst models of double vowel separation are not complete systems for source segregation, the emphasis on simultaneous organisation in single time-frames does not address the important concern of how the temporal organisation of auditory representations might be computed. As a consequence, systems such as that of Weintraub (which also seeks simultaneous organisation first) have to develop suitable post-grouping strategies to estimate the number and type of each source. Yet, mental representations of acoustic sources should result from the interplay of simultaneous and sequential organisation. Any model of these processes should be sufficiently flexible to allow incorporation of arbitrary grouping principles.

The title of this thesis stresses *organisation* rather than segregation. The emphasis of the model which has been developed has been to treat time and frequency as equally important dimensions in which organisation is sought. Hence, the initial stages of the model compute a time-frequency description of the signals which emanate from a model of the auditory periphery. Once such spectral and temporal correspondences have been made explicit, the resulting auditory scene is explored with the goal of integrating all those elements which are likely to have come from the same source. Although the model does not currently make use of many cues for organisation, the architecture can be extended to accommodate other grouping principles. As a result of the emphasis on organisation, it is not necessary to make unrealistic assumptions about the number or type of any sources present.

1.6 A guide to the thesis

The sequence of the thesis reflects the flow of processing in the model. Some of the representations and processes used are depicted in Figure 1.1.

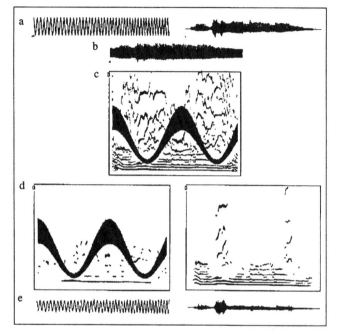

chapters

2: A model of the auditory periphery.

3: Auditory scene decomposition.

4: Modelling auditory scene exploration.

5: Implementation of auditory grouping principles.

6: Evaluation of sound source separation.

Figure 1.1 A representational guide to the thesis. *a*: speech and siren signals; *b*: mixture; *c*: synchrony strand representation for mixture; *d*: two groups of strands recovered; *e*: signals resynthesised from each group.

Chapters 2 and 3 describe the decomposition of a signal into a collection of objects - the auditory scene. Chapter 2 presents a detailed account of a model of the auditory periphery which extends recent work in filterbank modelling. Chapter 3 tackles the signal-to-symbol transformation required to make explicit the time-frequency structure in the auditory periphery outputs. The resulting representation - *synchrony strands*, shown as Figure 1.1(c,d) - attempts to capture the temporal evolution of synchronised filter responses.

Chapters 4 and 5 describe how the strand decomposition might be re-assembled. Chapter 4 explores computational issues in auditory scene analysis and defines a framework in which grouping principles can be embedded. Chapter 5 describes the specific grouping rules employed in this work, and reviews experimental evidence for their rôle in perceptual organisation.

Chapter 6 presents an evaluation of the model's ability to collect together material from one source or another. The evaluation is based on a database of 100 mixtures created by combining natural utterances with a variety of other sources. An example of the separate organisations discovered in one example from this collection is shown in Figure 1.1(d), together with waveforms resynthesised from each group.

2

The auditory periphery: physiology, function and a computer model

2.1 Introduction

In the past decade it has become routine for both modellers and experimenters to pass signals and stimuli through simulations of the peripheral auditory system, to the extent that such models are an essential tool for research in this area. One of the reasons for this new confidence in such models is the convergence of physiological and psychophysical estimates of auditory frequency selectivity, together with the appearance of computationally tractable models of hair cell function. Whilst most of the work described in this thesis is motivated by psychological investigation, there is some stability in physiologically-based modelling at the peripheral level.

Section 2.2 reviews the known physiology of mammalian peripheral auditory systems. Issues surrounding the selection of processing features to incorporate in a model are considered in section 2.3 in the light of several recent computational investigations. Section 2.4 introduces a new, 3-stage model of peripheral processing. The prospects for continued physiologically-based modelling beyond the periphery are considered in section 2.5.

2.2 The structure and function of the auditory periphery

The auditory system is functionally subdivided into the peripheral and the central. The boundary between the two is usually placed at the initial level of neural activity, the stimulation and generation of impulses in individual fibres of the auditory nerve. The boundary represents more than a purely anatomical division - it also represents a difference in our state of knowledge concerning the detailed operation of the two systems. The properties of the peripheral system are well known, even if all of the detailed underlying mechanisms are subject to debate. By contrast, we have few concrete notions about the methods by which the central auditory system is able to produce the known facts of hearing - the identification of complex stimulus properties, source attribution, and the formation of auditory space.

Overview

The ear can be divided into three zones - outer, middle and inner. The *outer* ear consists essentially of a cavity open to the external sound field and closed by the relatively stiff tympanic membrane. The *middle* ear region contains the ossicles - three small bones which are coupled to provide a mechanism for matching the impedance at the eardrum with that of the cochlear fluid.

Pressure variations in air travel through the outer ear to the tympanic membrane. This causes the sound to be transmitted via the ossicles of the middle ear to the oval window of the cochlea. The cochlea is a coiled, fluid-filled tube which is divided into two chambers along its length by the cochlear partition, and constitutes the *inner ear*. This partition includes the *basilar membrane* (BM) and the *organ of Corti*. Movement of the oval window creates pressure variations in the fluid surrounding the BM. The width and stiffness of the membrane vary monotonically along its length, with the widest and most flexible part being furthest away from the oval window. This combination of pressure variations and dimensional changes creates a travelling wave on the BM. For single frequency stimuli, starting from the oval window, the amplitude of BM displacement builds up to a maximum, then decreases rapidly. The position of the maximum depends on the frequency of the stimulating tone. High frequency waves are absorbed nearer to the oval window than low frequency ones. In this way, the envelope of BM displacement represents a spectral analysis of the signal, with frequency converted to place information.

The organ of Corti converts basilar membrane motion into nerve impulses by means of receptors known as hair cells, in a process called *hair cell transduction*. The amount of activity in a single auditory nerve fibre is nonlinearly related to the deflection of the hair bundles at the corresponding place in the organ of Corti.

The majority of auditory-nerve fibres innervate the inner hair cells. More numerous along the cochlear partition are the outer hair cells, whose properties have only recently been the subject of direct measurement.

Mechanical and tuning properties

The size of the mechanical response at a particular place on the BM as a function of stimulus frequency is called the *basilar membrane tuning curve*. Typical tuning curves show an asymmetric, bandpass characteristic, with very sharp high frequency cutoffs.

Several methods for obtaining BM tuning curves have been used (see Yates et al. [185] for a review), leading to some controversy regarding the sharpness of tuning. Initially, BM tuning was believed to be wider than that seen in single auditory nerve fibres. It now appears that the earlier measurements may have been influenced by BM damage, and Leonard and Khanna [104] have shown an inverse relationship between degree of damage and sharpness of tuning. It is generally accepted that the basilar membrane is capable of producing the fine frequency selectivity observed in auditory nerve fibre tuning curves.

As Yates [185] states:

> After more than two decades of attempts to correctly and accurately measure BM vibrations, it now seems that this goal has been achieved. (p.21)

Further strong arguments are put forward in Johnstone, Patuzzi and Yates [94]:

> The current consensus is that BM vibration is very sharply tuned, quite vulnerable to any insult and is the predominant determinant of the major responses of the eighth nerve, e.g. sensitivity, sharpness of tuning and many nonlinear functions. (p.148)

In an attempt to explain the measurements, it now seems probable that *active* cochlear mechanics are required. Several effects seem to require that energy be fed into the cochlear partition as a result of sound stimulation. For instance, the phenomenon known as *evoked cochlear mechanical response*, discovered by Kemp [98], manifests itself as a delayed wave recorded in the ear canal following presentation of a click stimulus. Later work suggested that this response has a cochlear origin, and Kemp calculated that more energy would sometimes be produced by the cochlea than had originally been introduced to it. In a different kind of study, de Boer [46] showed that, in order to match the sharpness of hair cell tuning curves, extra energy must be added by the membrane.

More recent results lend further support to the notion that BM mechanics has an active component. The experiments of Brownell et al. [20] and Ashmore [6] concern the mechanical properties of outer hair cells (OHC), whose properties had been largely unexplained. They showed that mammalian OHCs exhibit a change in length in response to a.c. stimulation, and conclude that this could lead to a change in stiffness of the BM and thus provide an additional mechanical contribution to BM dynamics. As Russell [145] states:

> The evidence that OHCs are the cellular elements responsible for the active
> hearing mechanisms is substantial, but circumstantial (p. 817)

Flock and Strelioff [61] report on the micromechanical properties of hair bundles. They suggest that the sharp frequency selectivity depends not only on the BM but also on the tuning and nonlinear properties of sensory hairs of receptor cells.

Hair cell transduction

The mechanical motion of the BM and cochlear partition cause changes in the electrical potentials present in the organ of Corti. Deflection of the hair bundles (stereocilia) of the inner hair cells produces a corresponding modulation of hair cell membrane potential, allowing current to flow through the cell. The depolarisation caused releases a chemical transmitter substance from the presynaptic region of the IHC. This substance diffuses across the synapse and is responsible for impulse generation in the attached auditory nerve fibre.

Russell [145] summarises the major properties of the IHC in relation to the BM and auditory nerve fibres:

> Membrane potentials of IHCs are modulated by the oscillatory movements of the
> stereocilia in response to tones presented at the tympanic membrane. The peak
> amplitude of this modulation can exceed 30mV and consists of a d.c. component
> which is always depolarizing and an a.c. component which alternates at the
> frequency of the stimulus. Both components are as sharply tuned as the transverse
> vibration of the basilar membrane, and the auditory nerve fibre responses in
> different turns of the cochlea. (p. 111)

Auditory nerve fibre responses

The activity in single auditory nerve fibres in response to sound has been studied extensively (e.g. Kiang, Watanabe, Thomas and Clark, [99]), and a number of properties have been described. Responses can be characterised in terms of frequency, level and temporal dependencies.

Neural tuning curves

One method used to measure single auditory nerve fibre responses is to count the number of impulses which occur in a time interval. This is called the *average rate* response. If the average rate is measured for a variety of frequencies of stimulating tones, a fibre tuning curve is obtained. Such curves show that each fibre has a frequency for which the response is maximal, called the *best frequency*. The tuning properties are rather sharp, indicating fine frequency selectivity. BM responses can now be shown to be as sharp as those of auditory nerve fibres, if an active BM mechanics is assumed.

Level dependence

Dependence of the response on stimulus level is usually measured at a fibre's best frequency. The result is called a *rate-intensity profile*, and is characterised by a sigmoidal shape. Fibres respond even in the absence of sound stimulation, at a rate called the *spontaneous rate*. In response to sound, the firing rate is initially constant until the stimulus intensity is large enough to overcome the spontaneous rate. It then increases approximately linearly with tone level, up to a point when the discharge rate is saturated. Further increases in stimulus intensity do not elicit increases in average rate past this point.

Temporal response

The rate response described above hides the fact that the average rate in response to, say, a tone burst, is not constant over time. Consideration of temporal properties is subdivided into two parts, the first dealing with envelope behaviour, the second with the fine structure of the response.

Average rate effects are generally revealed with the aid of a post-stimulus time histogram (PSTH). This histogram is derived by presenting a stimulus many times, and recording the times of occurrence of each spike relative to the onset of the stimulus. When a tone burst is used as the stimulus, the histogram shows an initial peak of activity, followed by a reduction in activity which is initially rapid, then slower. The activity asymptotically approaches a constant value, called the *adapted rate*, which is usually above the spontaneous level. At the offset of the tone burst, activity drops below the spontaneous rate, followed by a period of recovery back to the spontaneous rate.

Both the onset response and the adapted level for a particular fibre vary with stimulus level. Until recently, it was believed that the onset rate followed the same sigmoidal pattern with intensity as the adapted rate, albeit at a high level. This, however, presented difficulties in explaining how a wide range of sound pressure levels (up to 130 dB) could be encoded by the firing rates of auditory-nerve fibres, most of which have a dynamic range of less than 30 dB. However, recent analyses involving smaller time intervals in the production of the PSTH (Smith, Frisina and Goodman [169]) suggest that the onset rate continues to increase, even when the adapted rate has saturated.

Consider next the *fine time structure* of nerve responses for stimulus frequencies below 4-5 kHz. Fibre impulses show a distinct preference to discharge in a given half-cycle of the stimulating waveform, which will resemble a band-pass filtered version of the stimulus. This property can be seen in a form of display known as a *period histogram* [143], which is created by plotting the number of discharges in a time interval as a function of stimulus phase. It can be interpreted as measuring the probability of occurrence of a discharge at different points in a single cycle of the stimulus. Such histograms follow a half-wave rectified version of the stimulus waveform, and give rise to the term *phase-locked* response.

Phase-locked responses have some interesting properties. When the level of the stimulus is such that the average discharge rate is at the spontaneous level, the detailed response still shows phase-locking. Similarly, when the average rate is saturated, phase-locking is preserved. The facts have been used to explain how the fine structure may improve the representation of certain signals (Sachs, Voigt and Young [147]).

As an example, consider how a vowel might be encoded by the discharge rates in the array of auditory nerve fibres. One would expect to see peaks corresponding to peaks in the input spectrum. Suppose now that white noise is added to the vowel stimulus. This will have the effect of increasing the discharge rates of all fibres, thereby raising the baseline activity level. By increasing the level of the noise, all peaks will eventually disappear due to saturation, so the coding of the vowel spectrum will be lost. Yet psychophysical experiments (e.g. Scharf and Meiselman [149]) show that we clearly perceive vowel identity in such circumstances.

Various measures have been derived to quantify the synchronisation of fibre responses to particular stimulus components. One such measure is the *vector strength* indication of Johnson [92]. Since phase-locking occurs even at high levels of stimulation, vector strength is much less affected by background noise (Sachs, Voigt and Young [147]). Sinex and Geisler [164] compared the ability of average rate and discharge synchrony to represent synthetic speech stimuli. They found that a synchrony measure could provide a record of the precise trajectory of formants, even at high sound pressure levels.

It is not known whether the auditory system actually uses phase-locking information. Above 4-5 kHz, synchronisation becomes ragged and breaks down, requiring the use of average rate information at high frequencies. Certain types of units in the cochlear nucleus which may be able to extract timing information (Godfrey et al. [72]) have been identified.

2.3 Computer models of the auditory periphery

Although models of individual auditory processes such as BM filtering or hair-cell transduction go back to the late 60's and early 70's, few *integrated* models of the periphery appeared before the late 70's, exceptions being the models of Weiss [178] and Chistovitch [24]. These componential models were generally derived by researchers investigating the periphery, rather than workers interested in using an auditory model as a front-end for a speech recogniser. An exception to this was the work of Dolmazon et al. [51]. The situation changed dramatically in the early 80's, when a succession of multistage models were developed by workers with a mainly engineering interest. Perhaps the most influential model was that of Lyon (successively described in [110] [111] [112] [113]), brought to a wide audience through the International Conference of Acoustics, Speech and Signal Processing. In fairly rapid succession, most major speech laboratories were working on, or using, auditory models.

In general, these models did not use detailed simulations of specific peripheral processes, but concentrated on 'engineering solutions' - i.e. on model components which reproduced many of the main effects of some peripheral process. For instance, rather than provide a detailed mathematical simulation of the basilar membrane and associated structures, the systems action as a filterbank would be modelled, using filterbank parameters derived either from psychoacoustic studies (e.g. ERB, Bark or mel scale) or from physiological investigation (e.g. best-frequency to place mapping, Liberman [107]). Similarly, the model of temporal adaptation often used (e.g. Lyon [110]; Seneff [156]) would involve some form of AGC. This overall approach is pragmatically motivated - we simply do not understand sufficiently the detailed processes involved, in, say, the mechanical filtering action of the BM and proximate structures to derive a detailed simulation.

More recent models have addressed both computational pragmatism with the desire to model peripheral processes in more detail than the earlier systems. As an example, models which incorporate nonlinear basilar membrane dynamics are starting to appear (e.g. Deng et al. [50]). Deng et al. debate the importance of these effects for the representation of speech:

> Our model suggests that this nonlinearity is crucial for producing the detailed
> spatio-temporal discharge patterns characteristic of auditory nerve fibre responses
> to speech (p. 94).

However, not all effects are common in auditory models. For instance, few published models[†] include responses of low spontaneous discharge rate fibres, whose behaviour is far more variable than their high spontaneous rate neighbours, yet whose action may be important for encoding speech in a rate representation (Shofner and Sachs [163]; Sachs, Blackburn and Young [148]).

Other examples of selectivity in which aspects to model occur in the following statements:

> The model omits certain properties of auditory-nerve function for the sake of
> economy. By modelling the nerve-fibre firing activity as a point process produced
> by a level-crossing detector, the probabilistic nature of the neural firing
> mechanism is essentially neglected ... The adaptation of nerve-fibre discharge
> (Smith and Zwislocki, [166]) is also omitted from the model. This omission may

---

† Delgutte's model [49] contains rate-intensity nonlinearities corresponding to 3 fibre populations.

not affect the basic representation since the amount of adaptation is reduced considerably in the presence of noise, even in such noise levels where human performance is still high (Sachs, Voigt and Young, [147]). If it is assumed that the operation of the central auditory pathway remains constant over a wide range of acoustic conditions, it is likely that the information conveyed by rate adaptation may not play a significant rôle in the processing of speech. (Ghitza [70], p. 113)

Other important cochlear mechanisms include adaptation at the inner-hair-cell/ auditory-nerve fibre synapse (Westerman and Smith [180]; Geisler [68]; Seneff [159]), the efferent system (Winslow [183]) and the influence of the middle-ear (staepedius and tensor tympani) muscles on the function of an automatic-gain-control mechanism. Despite the omission of these components, the present model is capable of reproducing the major response properties of auditory-nerve fibres and is probably adequate for describing the peripheral auditory response (Shamma [160][161]) to relatively steady-state and broadband stimuli, such as the vowels and voiceless fricatives examined in the present study. (Shamma [162], p. 79)

Evidently, there is no consensus on the question of which components are of sufficient importance to model, and justification for the particular choice must reside with the modeller. Reasons for leaving components out include a lack of relevant physiological data, or aspects subject to controversy, or perhaps no necessity given the experimental purpose of model. Ultimately, models must be judged on the basis of their intended use. A model which serves to replace animals in physiological investigation must follow the physiology rather more slavishly than one intended as a front-end for an automatic speech recogniser. The model proposed in this chapter is designed to support the grouping activities which are described in chapters 4 and 5.

In order to place the periphery model described in the next section into the context of existing models, a qualitative comparison between its characteristics with those of some recent models is provided in Table 2.1 which compares the basilar membrane[†], IHC nonlinearity[‡] and adaptation[#] stages and the form of output produced[††].

2.4 A model of the auditory periphery

Outline

In common with many of the auditory models described in the previous section, the model consists of a number of parallel, frequency specific channels, each of which models the behaviour of the auditory system at some point along the basilar membrane, together with proximate struc-

---

†. Generally, entries fall into the category of filter bank (FB) or transmission line (TL). Filterbank implementations make use of filters with magnitude (and sometimes phase) responses designed to match physiological data. Other possibilities reflected in the table are frequency domain implementations, which manipulate spectra directly, or impulse response convolution, as used by Evans. Transmission line models tend to be 1-dimensional, and are usually implemented as a cascade of filter sections.

‡. This stage is designed to reflect the conversion of stereocilia displacement to IHC d.c. receptor potential. Models here range from ideal half-wave rectifiers (Lyon, Evans) to static nonlinearities with some physiological justification (Seneff, Deng).

#. The main distinguishing feature of models of the time course of adaptation of spike rate in single auditory nerve fibres is the ability of the model to reproduce additive responses as seen in the data of, for example, Smith and Zwislocki [166]. Simpler models function like an automatic gain control.

††. Here, some indication of the usual form which the output takes is given. This may be spike trains (like the auditory nerve), spike probabilities (like post-stimulus time histograms), some hybrid scheme (joint synchrony/rate measures) or a specific representation associated with the model (e.g. Seneff's synchrony spectrogram, Shamma's output from a lateral inhibitory network (LIN), Ghitza's ensemble interval histogram (EIH) or Deng's pseudo spectrum derived by cross correlation).

Table 2.1: Characteristics of some recent auditory models.

model	basilar membrane	IHC nonlinearity	adaptation	output
Delgutte [49]	FB Kiang/Moxon [100]	sigmoid Liberman [106]		spike probability
Deng et al. [50]	TL Viergever [174]	ogive Hudspeth/Corey [88]	AGC Oonu/Sujaku [130]	pseudo-spectrum
Dolmazon et al. [51]	TL Chistovich [24]		coupled AGC	lateral inhibition network
Evans [57]	revcor de Boer/ Kuyper [44]	rectifier, AGC, LPF	AGC Shroeder/Hall [152]	spike trains
Ghitza [70]	FB Allen [4]	multiple level-crossings		ensemble interval histogram
Goldhor [73]	freq. domain Patterson [132]	raised hyperbolic tangent	additive	spike probability
Lyon [110]	TL Zweig et al. [189]	half-wave rectifier	2 stage coupled AGC	spike probability
Seneff [159]	FB ad hoc	arctangent	additive Goldhor [73]	synchrony spectrum
Shamma [161]	TL Holmes/Cole [86]	sigmoid		lateral inhibition network
current model	FB Patterson et al. [133]	bilinear Crawford/Fettiplace [31]	additive state-partition model	instantaneous frequency & envelope

tures. A single channel of the model has three stages, depicted in Figure 2.1:

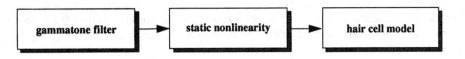

Figure 2.1 A single channel of the periphery model.

- a *filter* with impulse response designed to match physiological data;
- a *saturating static nonlinearity* whose shape is derived from recordings of inner hair cell potentials, and
- a *hair cell transmitter depletion model* which reproduces most of the physiological results relating to the *rate* response of auditory-nerve fibres.

The gammatone filterbank

History

In 1968, de Boer and Kuyper [44] developed a system identification method (which they called 'triggered correlation', but which is better known as 'reverse correlation'), which allows the impulse response of an auditory nerve fibre to be calculated. Briefly, the method is based on the notion that auditory nerve fibre discharges are correlated with the input stimulus, albeit via an unknown system. If the unknown system is linear (or some suitable assumptions are made), then knowledge of the stimulus just prior to the initiated spike can lead to a quantitative estimate of the impulse response of the unknown system.

For computational purposes, it is desirable to have an analytic expression for the experimentally derived impulse response[†]. An expression which fits the nerve data well (de Boer and de Jongh [45]) is the *gammatone*[‡] function:

$$g(t) = t^{n-1} e^{-bt} \cos(\omega t) u(t) \tag{1}$$

Here, n is the filter order, b is related to bandwidth, ω is the radian centre frequency and $u(t)$ is the unit-step sequence (i.e. $u(t) = 1$ for positive t, 0 otherwise).

Renewed interest in the gammatone filter as a suitable BM filtering model has been shown by a number of researchers, notably Schofield [151], Holdsworth et al. [85] and Evans [58]. Schofield demonstrated that the gammatone function of order 4 provides a very close fit to the human auditory filter shapes derived by Patterson [132], and presented some displays resulting from a bank of gammatone filters. Patterson et al. [133] extended Schofield's analysis to take account of more recent analytic fits (the rounded exponential family) to human auditory filter shapes derived psychophysically. They show that a 4th order gammatone filter provides an extremely good fit to the simplest (one-parameter) member of the rounded-exponential family (so-called roex(p)), over a 60 dB range. They conclude that:

> the gammatone filter offers a means of producing an auditory filterbank that is in excellent agreement with both physiological and psychophysical data on frequency selectivity. (p. 8)

Holdsworth et al. [85] presented a recursive digital implementation of a gammatone filterbank which provides a very efficient route for a model of BM filtering action. In this implementation, a pole-mapping technique is used to convert from the continuous domain gammatone response to the digital domain.

An alternative implementation of an auditory model using data from reverse correlation experiments has been reported by Evans [57][58]. He used a digital implementation of a finite impulse response filter (the Institute for Hearing Research FIR Filter, Trinder [173]) which allows an arbitrary amplitude and phase spectrum, with actual reverse correlation data (as opposed to the analytic gammatone expression) loaded. The main disadvantage in using this technique is its computational expense.

In summary, the gammatone filter serves as a bridge between auditory physiology and auditory psychophysics so far as frequency selectivity is concerned. Primary data comes from the level of the auditory nerve rather than the basilar membrane; as such, any sharpness of tuning contributed by nonlinearities in BM mechanics will be incorporated into the measured response at the nerve level.

---

†. Although the actual 'raw' nerve data could be used in truncated form in an FIR filter, as in the work of Evans [58].

‡. According to de Boer and Kruidenier [47], the phrase 'gamma tone' was proposed originally by Aertsen and Johannesma [1].

A new approach to gammatone filterbank implementation

The approach taken here is to examine in some detail the form of digital approximation used to derive an implementable gammatone filter. As described earlier, Holdsworth et al. [85] use a pole-mapping technique to convert from the continuous to discrete domain. This is not the only method possible. In fact, it is often the case that pole-mapping can lead to poor representations of one or more of the characteristic responses of a linear system - magnitude, impulse and phase. It is therefore of interest to compare other approximation techniques with the ideal form of each response.

The task of digital filter design in general involves determining a z-domain system transfer function (or equivalently, the coefficients of the difference equation) given some filter specification in the continuous domain. For linear systems, the continuous domain property may be represented either by the transfer function or the impulse response - both fully characterise the system. For the gammatone function discussed above, we start from an analytic expression for the impulse response.

A number of digital approximations are available in order to derive the discrete equivalent of a continuous-time filter. In general, we must select the transformation which leads to a digital filter best approximating some aspect of the system - usually the magnitude, phase or impulse response. It is extremely important to evaluate the results of digital approximation, since we cannot rely on all methods to accurately reproduce the characteristics specified by the continuous domain transfer function or impulse response.

Following Holdsworth et al., the following discussion assumes that filters are implemented according to a frequency-shifting method outlined below:

- frequency shift input data by an amount corresponding to the centre frequency of the filter, ω.
- apply the low-pass gammatone filter, $g_{lp}(t) = t^{n-1}e^{-bt}$
- frequency shift back to the centre frequency region.

This simplifies the task to one of finding a digital approximation to the system with impulse response

$$g_{lp}(t) = t^{n-1}e^{-bt}u(t) \tag{2}$$

The three digital approximation techniques used were pole-mapping, bilinear transform and impulse invariant transform.

Pole-mapping. In the pole-mapping technique, poles and zeros of the continuous domain transfer function are individually transformed into z-plane poles and zeros using the relationship

$$z = e^{sT} \tag{3}$$

where $s = j\omega$ and T is the sampling interval.

Bilinear transform. The bilinear transform method of digital approximation is a widely used technique which effectively compresses the whole of the imaginary axis in the s-plane into a single revolution of the unit circle in the z-plane, with everything in the left-half s-plane mapping inside the z-plane unit circle.

Impulse invariant transform. This method is derived from the observation that, in order to preserve the response of the analogue system to an impulse, the transfer function in the digital domain should be transformable into a sampled version of the actual impulse response.

Complete gammatone derivations for each of these methods can be found in Appendix 1, sections 1-3. It is possible to derive general (i.e. order-independent) expressions for the z-domain system function for both bilinear and pole-mapping techniques.

Comparisons

Since the gammatone filter is available in analytic form, it is possible to compare various filter properties such as magnitude, phase and impulse responses, across the different implementations, with respect to the analytic form. In order to do this, the reference responses are required, as are formulae which enable calculation of digital filter characteristics. These are derived in Appendix 1, sections 4 and 5 respectively.

In the discussion below, it is assumed that data sequences $\{x_i\}$, $\{y_i\}$ represent the pair of responses being compared. In each case, $\{x_i\}$ represents the 'ideal' response, whether it be magnitude, phase or impulse, whilst $\{y_i\}$ is the corresponding response of either the pole-mapped, bilinear or impulse invariant filter.

Initially, comparisons were based on computing the unbiased correlation coefficient of the data sequences $\{x_i\},\{y_i\}$, as defined by

$$\rho = \frac{\sum (x_i - \bar{x})(y_i - \bar{y})}{\sqrt{\sum (x_i - \bar{x})^2 (y_i - \bar{y})^2}} \tag{4}$$

It is of interest to see how the three approximation methods compare as a function of centre frequency and filter order. Four centre frequencies (100, 1000, 5000 and 8000 Hz) and four filter orders (1-4) were used. Additionally, in the case of magnitude and phase responses, the frequency extent over which the correlation is performed will affect the results. As the extent is increased, more of the filter skirt is taken into account. Therefore, comparisons were made over the frequency extents necessary to gain 30, 60 and 120 dB attenuation. For the impulse response, it makes sense to perform the correlation only over the region where the response is of a reasonable size. For example, the impulse response in the case of very high frequencies takes on significant values for the first few tens of samples. Performing the correlation over a much larger range will lead to overly optimistic results since most of the time the two responses will be near to zero and well correlated. To get round this problem, the comparison is over the interval $[0, t_{crit}]$, where t_{crit} is the sample at which the impulse response has decayed to some fraction of its peak value - the value of 1% has been chosen here.

Since many of the correlations are near to unity, a more intuitive notion of similarity is desirable. What does a correlation of 0.99 mean in terms of, for example, the magnitude response? A more intuitive estimate can be based on the mean error between the two responses. This has the more comprehensible units of decibels. Similarly, phase and impulse response errors are easier to appreciate when measured in this way. In the tables below, figures in parentheses are mean error measures.

Magnitude response

Table 2.2 presents the magnitude response correlations and mean errors for the three approximation techniques as the order of the filter is varied from 1 to 4 (centre frequency: 8 kHz, range: 60 dB). No strong dependence on order is found, though there is a tendency for higher order filters

Table 2.2: The effect of filter order on magnitude response correlation.

order	pole-mapping	bilinear	impulse invariant
1	0.994 (1.254)	0.904 (4.711)	0.994 (1.254)
2	0.993 (2.501)	0.906 (9.262)	0.993 (2.501)
3	0.993 (3.695)	0.936 (12.58)	0.998 (0.995)
4	0.998 (2.126)	0.994 (4.424)	0.999 (0.043)

to be more accurate. Both pole-mapping and impulse invariant filters have lower errors than the bilinear transform technique for all orders, whilst impulse invariance significantly outperforms the other two methods at filter orders 3 and 4. It is of interest to note that large values of the correlation coefficient can be somewhat misleading. For example, the 4th order pole-mapped and impulse invariant filters have very similar correlations, yet the pole-mapped response has a mean error of more than 2 dB (over a 60 dB range), whilst the impulse invariant method has a negligible error (less than 0.05 dB).

Table 2.3 illustrates the effect of varying filter centre frequency. Here, a 4th order filter with a range of 60 dB was chosen. There is a reduction in accuracy with increasing centre frequency, as might be expected of these design methods (Ludeman [114]). For low CF, all methods are very accurate. However, at higher frequencies, both bilinear and pole-mapping begin to show mean errors of a few decibels, whilst the impulse invariant method maintains accuracy.

Table 2.3: The effect of filter centre frequency on magnitude response correlation.

centre frequency	pole-mapping	bilinear	impulse invariant
100	1.000 (0.002)	1.000 (0.004)	1.000 (0.000)
1000	1.000 (0.025)	0.999 (0.044)	1.000 (0.000)
5000	0.999 (0.648)	0.999 (1.173)	1.000 (0.003)
8000	0.998 (2.126)	0.994 (4.424)	0.999 (0.043)

Table 2.4 completes the consideration of magnitude responses by presenting the effect of frequency extent over which the comparison is made. Here, a 4th order filter with the highest cen-

Table 2.4: The effect of attenuation range on magnitude response correlation.

attenuation (dB)	pole-mapping	bilinear	impulse invariant
30	0.999 (0.316)	0.999 (0.296)	1.000 (0.001)
60	0.998 (2.126)	0.994 (4.424)	0.999 (0.043)
120	0.992 (4.976)	0.965 (14.72)	0.999 (0.654)

tre frequency was chosen as representing the worst case. However, other orders and CFs followed the same pattern. A clear effect of reduction in accuracy with extent is observed. Again, this is expected since the design techniques effectively concentrate the fitting accuracy around the critical points (poles and zeros). The impulse invariant technique again outperforms the other methods.

To properly visualise the differences between the three methods and the ideal, Figure 2.2 illustrates the four magnitude responses for a 4th order filter with centre frequency of 8 kHz. All filters provide a close fit to the ideal over the first 15 dB; after this, first the bilinear, then the pole-mapped response diverge from the ideal, whilst the impulse invariant magnitude response stays very close to the ideal for the first 60 dB.

Phase response

Similar effects of filter order, centre frequency and extent can be seen for (unwrapped) phase responses, some of which are shown in Figure 2.2. Table 2.5 illustrates typical results for the phase response (filter order: 4, range: 60 dB). Here, the effect of variation in centre frequency is presented.

phase responses

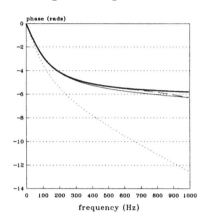

impulse responses

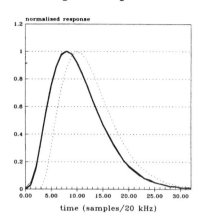

magnitude responses

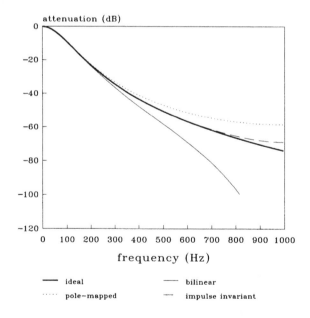

Figure 2.2 Magnitude, phase and impulse responses for a 4th order gammatone filter (lowpass) with centre frequency of 8 kHz.

Table 2.5: The effect of filter centre frequency on phase response correlation.

centre frequency	pole-mapping	bilinear	impulse invariant
100	0.999 (0.069)	1.000 (0.000)	1.000 (0.000)
1000	0.999 (0.230)	1.000 (0.001)	1.000 (0.000)
5000	0.987 (1.196)	0.999 (0.032)	1.000 (0.000)
8000	0.972 (2.218)	0.999 (0.111)	0.999 (0.010)

Mean errors are measured in radians in this table. Pole-mapped phase responses show quite large mean errors at high centre frequencies, whilst those of bilinear and impulse invariant responses are quite small. As with the magnitude response, the impulse invariant technique outperforms the other two.

Impulse response

Impulse response correlations for variation in filter order is shown in Table 2.6, for a filter with 8 kHz centre frequency. As with magnitude responses, no strong effect of filter order is visible.

Table 2.6: The effect of filter order on impulse response correlation.

order	pole-mapping	bilinear	impulse invariant
1	0.809 (0.048)	0.951 (0.035)	1.000 (0.000)
2	0.945 (0.058)	0.997 (0.007)	1.000 (0.000)
3	0.916 (0.093)	0.999 (0.004)	0.999 (0.009)
4	0.869 (0.126)	0.999 (0.005)	1.000 (0.000)

Finally, impulse response correlations for variation in filter centre frequency are shown in Table 2.7. Responses get poorer with filter centre frequency. Impulse invariance gives nearly per-

Table 2.7: The effect of filter centre frequency on impulse response correlation.

centre frequency	pole-mapping	bilinear	impulse invariant
100	0.999 (0.004)	1.000 (0.000)	1.000 (0.000)
1000	0.998 (0.014)	1.000 (0.000)	1.000 (0.000)
5000	0.960 (0.071)	0.999 (0.001)	1.000 (0.000)
8000	0.869 (0.126)	0.999 (0.005)	1.000 (0.000)

fect responses for all conditions, whilst pole-mapping is least accurate.

Figure 2.2 reveals that the poor performance of the pole-mapping technique is due mainly to a phase shift relative to the ideal response. A delay of approximately 2 samples (at 20 kHz) brings the responses into alignment. This sort of discrepancy is to be expected from a method with simply transfers poles from the continuous to the discrete domain, since it produces a spurious set of zeroes (see below).

Analysis of results

It is clear from the above comparisons that, of the three methods of digital approximation used in this study, the impulse invariant transform provides the best match to ideal magnitude, phase and impulse responses. This is a little unexpected. Digital filter design texts usually consider a method such as the bilinear transform to provide close fits to the magnitude response, for instance, and often claim that impulse invariance, whilst performing its task of accurately matching the desired impulse response, will tend to produce poor magnitude characteristics. However, this statement applies particularly when the filter has critical frequencies near to the Nyquist frequency. Since the filters here are lowpass, with the bandpass response being achieved by a frequency shifting technique, the critical frequencies are, at most, one tenth of the Nyquist frequency.

A consideration of the pole locations shows that both pole-mapped and impulse invariant filters have identical z-plane poles. Hence, the improvement in accuracy shown by impulse invariance is achieved by proper positioning of the zeros, rather than the forced positioning implied by simply mapping poles from the s- to z-planes.

How significant are the inaccuracies between the methods? For the magnitude response, all methods provide a good fit over the first 20 dB. However, it *may* be important to correctly reject components some way from the centre frequency in order to provide some degree of noise robustness. Here, the pole-mapped response is providing between 2 and 6 dB less attenuation than the ideal, whilst the bilinear response provides 5-20 dB too much.

Impulse response discrepancies are potentially important to any later processing which calculates synchrony information from the fine temporal filter output (as described in Chapter 3). However, the three methods provide a very close fit to the impulse response envelope, allowing for a phase-shifting correction to the pole-mapped response. It is more difficult to assess the importance of differences in phase response, since the gammatone phase response does not necessarily correspond to the auditory phase response. The auditory response is generally held to continue over a number of radians (Rhode [141]).

As a result of this comparison, the impulse invariant design method of digital approximation was used in all further work with the filterbank.

Hair cell static nonlinearity

The output of the gammatone filter represents the basilar membrane displacement with time at a particular place along the membrane.

Basilar membrane displacement causes deflection of the stereocilia which in turn modulate the IHC receptor potential. This has been studied in turtles (Crawford and Fettiplace [31]), guinea pigs (Sellick and Russell [155]), and frogs (Hudspeth and Corey [88]). Stereocilia displacement or shear (Ashmore [6]) is measured and plotted against receptor potential. The effect of this appears to be a static nonlinearity imposed *prior* to neurotransmitter release, and could explain the sigmoidal shape of auditory nerve fibre rate-intensity functions.

Most modellers assume some sigmoidal shape for the nonlinearity; for example, Seneff [159] uses an inverse tangent, Shamma [162] has a sigmoidal function, whilst Meddis has, successively, a bilinear [119] or log [121] expression. These authors claim various physiological motivations for their choice. Ross [144], whilst not explicitly using any physiological justification, utilises an approximation to the BM displacement versus rate intensity curve given in Sachs and Abbas [146].

There are few analytic expressions provided by physiologists to describe the shape of this nonlinearity. It is therefore a little surprising that the expression given by Crawford and Fettiplace has been overlooked by most modellers. The expression relating stimulus sound pressure x to inner hair cell receptor potential y is given by

$$y = y_0 + y_m \left(\frac{x}{x + \bar{x}} \right) \qquad x > 0 \tag{5}$$

together with a similar form suitable for negative x (which is not required here).

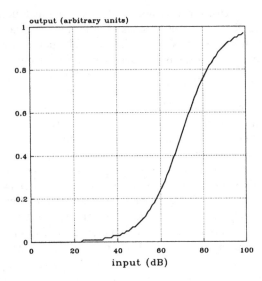

output (arbitrary units)

input (dB)

Figure 2.3 The static linearity plotted on a decibel scale. The shape resembles that of the rate-intensity function measured at stimulus onset.

If this is used as the static nonlinearity and plotted on a *decibel* scale, the resulting curve (see Figure 2.3) looks very similar to the unadapted rate intensity functions of, for example, Smith and Brachman [168]. This supports the hypothesis that the onset response is not subject to further saturation.

Using the Crawford and Fettiplace formula (5), it is unnecessary to 'hand-craft' the onset response in the way of, for instance, Smith and Brachman [168] who say:

> The immediate store was designed to produce rapid adaptation with additive incremental responses and *any desired unadapted rate-intensity function.* (my italics) (p. 111)

and later:

> The expression consists of the steady-state rate-intensity function developed by Zwislocki [190] plus an ad hoc slope to produce the sloping asymptote of the unadapted function at higher intensities. (p. 118)

The Crawford and Fettiplace expression is used for the second stage of the model described here, due to its ability to explain the shape of the neural rate-intensity curves.

It is possible to reinterpret (5) in terms of auditory nerve fibre rate-intensity relations by associating y_0 with the spontaneous discharge rate, y_m with the peak spike rate, and by choosing x as an input value causing half-saturation. It is useful to normalise the response by setting $y_0 = 0$, $y_m = 1$. A value of $x = 100$ gives reasonable rate-intensity curves, assuming that a signal amplitude of 1 corresponds to 30 dB (an assumption often made, e.g. Schroeder and Hall [152]; Meddis [119]).

Hair cell model

The final stage of the model is designed to reflect the hair cell to nerve fibre stage of auditory analysis. It is generally held that the adaptation of nerve fibre firing rate is caused by depletion of neurotransmitter immediately prior to the synapse. Early attempts at modelling adaptation used a single store, or reservoir, of transmitter (Schroeder and Hall [152]; Oonu and Sujaku [130]). These are described as multiplicative systems, or automatic gain controls, since depletion causes a reduced gain factor for the whole system. Actual measurements (e.g. Smith and Zwislocki [166]) of nerve fibre responses to tones of differing intensities indicate that multiplicative models are unable to reproduce some of the main adaptation effects. One such effect is additivity, in which the change in response produced by an increment in stimulus level is independent of the amount of prior adaptation. Duifhuis and Bezemer [55] examined the implications of a multiplicative model in predicting psychophysical temporal masking, and concluded that the multiplicative model was untenable.

More recent models (e.g. Smith and Brachman [168]; Schwid and Geisler [153]) attempted to incorporate additive effects using multiple reservoir systems. Each reservoir has its own *sensitivity threshold*, which indicates the stimulus level required for that reservoir to become effective. In this way, an increment in level causes undepleted reservoirs to contribute. Supporting physiological evidence for multiple release sites has come from Furukawa et al. [63]. They performed a statistical analysis of transmitter release at the hair cell to afferent fibre synapse in the goldfish sacculus. They found that the size of the available store of transmitter increased, rather than the release probability, with an increase in stimulus level. This effect can be explained by the presence of multiple release sites, with each site releasing a constant fraction of its contents.

Multiple reservoir systems, such as that of Smith and Brachman [168], are able to reproduce most of the observed effects of the hair cell to nerve fibre transduction process, including additivity. However, these are generally computational complex[†]. For example, Smith and Brachman's model simulates 512 neurotransmitter release sites for each hair cell. An implementation for a whole filterbank is prohibitive. However, it is possible, starting from the same assumptions about graded release sites, to produce a computationally efficient model which preserves most of the useful properties, especially additivity. A first attempt at this was reported in Cooke [27]. That model, however, made some unrealistic assumptions about transmitter replenishment which turn out to be unnecessary. Here, the transmitter replenishment strategy is modified. The new model is described below.

A State Partition Model of hair cell to nerve fibre transduction

The State Partition Model (SPM) attempts to characterise the dynamic properties of a population of transmitter release sites, each of which releases a constant fraction of its contents whenever the stimulus level is sufficient to activate it. In this respect, it is motivated by the Smith and Brachman [168] model.

Suppose the release sites are ordered by increasing sensitivity threshold. Each site is subject to either depletion or replenishment of transmitter, or both. These three cases are distinguished as follows:

1. If the current stimulus level is sufficiently high to activate the site, it undergoes depletion of its contents and receives replacement transmitter.
2. If the sensitivity threshold of the site is higher than the current stimulus level, it is not depleted. However, if it has been depleted in the recent past, it continues to be replenished.
3. If the site has not been active in the recent past, it is neither depleted nor replenished.

Since sites are ordered by sensitivity, all sites in the first condition will form a contiguous group, separate from those which behave according to the second condition, which in turn is distinct from those falling under condition 3. Therefore, the population of release sites are considered as being partitioned into 3 groups, or states, which are labelled *immediate*, *relax* and *reserve*.

There is no computational advantage in modelling each release site, since that implies having to keep track of its transmitter concentration and sensitivity threshold. Instead, by partitioning

---

[†]. An exception is the reuptake model of Meddis [121].

the population into a small number of states as described above, individual sites can be ignored; instead it is sufficient to model the three states.

A formal definition of the State Partition Model

Two variables describe each state, one representing the fraction of release sites represented by that state, the other denoting the average concentration of substance over all sites in that state[†]. These variables are represented by

$$v_s(t), c_s(t) \qquad s \in \{imm, rel, res\}$$

The fraction of release sites immediately available for depletion, $v_{\text{imm}}(t)$, is determined solely by the stimulus input level. An invariant (6) can be used to state that sites in the reserve state have not been active in the recent past.

$$\forall t \qquad c_{res}(t) = 1 \tag{6}$$

The reserve state consists of sites which have never been depleted, together with sites transferred from the relax state when they become full.

Depletion is modelled in accordance with physiological data (e.g. Furukawa et al. [63]), in which it is assumed that the fraction of transmitter released from each active site is constant. Since only sites in the immediate state are available for depletion, the time-varying output of this stage of the auditory model is given by

$$kv_{imm}(t)\, c_{imm}(t) \tag{7}$$

where k is the *release fraction.*

A simple, single-stage replenishment strategy is provided (for reasons which are discussed later). This assumes that a single source of replacement transmitter substance is available. In common with most other hair-cell models, the amount of transmitter replaced is determined by the uni-directional concentration gradient between the source and destination. For the State Partition Model, all sites which have undergone depletion in the recent past are subject to replenishment, which in turn requires that both the immediate and relax states receive replacement transmitter.

The amounts of transmitter received by the immediate and relax states are given by

$$l(1 - c_{imm}(t)) \tag{8}$$

and

$$l(1 - c_{rel}(t)) \tag{9}$$

where l is the *replenishment fraction* and the concentration in the replacement store is assumed to be constant and equal to unity.

To complete the description of the State Partition Model, it is necessary to describe the movement of transmitter between partitions, or, equivalently, the change in location of partition boundaries. Since the fraction of sites in the immediate state, $v_{imm}(t)$, is equal to the input stimulus level, the partition location changes only when there is a change in stimulus level. The two cases of rise and fall in level are considered separately.

For a rise in stimulus level, the fraction of release sites increases by recruiting sites from either or both the relax and reserve states. Whether or not it is necessary to recruit sites from both states is dependent on the size of the increment. If sufficient sites are available in the relax state, then these are recruited. Otherwise, all relax sites and sufficient reserve sites to make up the

---

†. Using normalised rather than quantised values for these variables provides for a simpler exposition of the model's properties, and lends itself to the use of the normalised static nonlinearity described in eqn. (5).

shortfall are transferred. Transmitter concentrations are assumed to equalise instantaneously. The details for the various cases are given below, assuming a stimulus level of $x(t)$ and time step of δt.

$$\text{Case I: } x(t) > v_{imm}(t) + v_{rel}(t) \tag{10}$$

$$c_{imm}(t + \delta t) = \frac{1}{x(t)} [c_{imm}(t) v_{imm}(t) + c_{rel}(t) v_{rel}(t) + x(t) - v_{rel}(t) - v_{imm}(t)]$$

$$\text{Case II: } x(t) \leq v_{imm}(t) + v_{rel}(t) \tag{11}$$

$$c_{imm}(t + \delta t) = \frac{1}{x(t)} [c_{imm}(t) v_{imm}(t) + c_{rel}(t) (x(t) - v_{imm}(t))]$$

For a stimulus level decrease, sites which previously were depleted are placed in the relax state. Concentration in the immediate state remains unaltered, but concentration in the relax state instantaneously adjusts itself according to the following expression:

$$c_{rel}(t + \delta t) = \frac{c_{imm}(t) [v_{imm}(t) - x(t)] + v_{rel}(t) c_{rel}(t)}{v_{imm}(t) + v_{rel}(t) - x(t)} \tag{12}$$

Properties of the State Partition Model
In this section, various properties of the State Partition Model are derived. Whilst it is not possible to give analytic expressions for the model output given arbitrary input, it is possible to derive exact model responses for constant input levels. This allows sensible estimation of parameters and gives a very full account of model behaviour without recourse to actual simulation, in contrast to most accounts of hair-cell models. Of course, actual responses produced by the model have been tested against the theoretical forms discussed below; both produce identical results. Details of all derivations are given in Appendix 2.

Response to a constant input. For constant input (i.e. constant stimulus envelope) of magnitude x, the rate of change of concentration in the immediate state is given by

$$\frac{dc_{imm}}{dt} = -kxc_{imm} + l(1 - c_{imm}) \tag{13}$$

It may be shown (Appendix 2) that the solution to this first order differential equation is

$$c_{imm} = \frac{l}{\lambda} + (1 - \frac{l}{\lambda}) e^{-\lambda t} \tag{14}$$

where $\lambda = kx + l$.
Hence, the time course of adaptation has an exponential decay, as required and expected of a single reservoir model. Furthermore, the adapted rate can be found as $kxc_{imm}(\infty)$, which is $\frac{kxl}{\lambda}$.

The time constant of adaptation is

$$\tau_{adapt} = -\frac{1}{kx + l} ln\frac{1}{2} \tag{15}$$

Recovery to spontaneous rate. After prolonged stimulation, a stimulus offset (to zero) will leave the immediate store in a depleted state. The differential equation describing transmitter concentration is given below:

$$\frac{dc_{imm}}{dt} = l(1 - c_{imm}) \tag{16}$$

whose solution is

$$c_{imm} = 1 - \frac{kx}{kx+l}e^{-lt} \tag{17}$$

As t approaches infinity, the concentration returns to unity. The time constant for recovery is

$$\tau_{recovery} = -\frac{1}{l}ln\frac{1}{2} \tag{18}$$

which is therefore independent of the previous level of stimulation.

Response to a stimulus increment. Perhaps the main motivation for the model form described above is its ability to replicate envelope behaviour of the auditory response when presented with an increment in stimulus level. This section shows how the model response can be derived (analytically) and compares this with physiological results.

First, let x_1, x_2 be the pre- and post-increment stimulus levels. After the static nonlinearity described above, these become y_1, y_2. The incremental response can be written as

$$increment = k(y_2c_2 - y_1c_1) \tag{19}$$

where c_1, c_2 represent the values of c_{imm} before and after the increment.

Due to the way in which the concentration in the immediate state changes when faced with a stimulus increment[†], we can write

$$c_2 = \frac{c_1y_1 + (y_2 - y_1)}{y_2} \tag{20}$$

which, when substituted into the expression above leads to

$$increment = k(y_2 - y_1) \tag{21}$$

This, of course, assumes $y_2 \neq 0$ (which holds here since $y_2 > y_1$).

The amount of increment, then, is *exactly* the same as that produced by an increment at stimulus onset. Hence, the model has an exact additive property, and, further, this fact can be ascertained by analysis rather than simulation.

The shape of the rate increment versus pedestal intensity curve (for a given size of stimulus increment), corresponds to computing the difference in the output of the static nonlinearity (5) over a step equal to the stimulus increment. Figure 2.4 shows incremental and decremental responses.

Response to a stimulus decrement. By a similar analysis, it is possible to arrive at an expression for the change in rate in response to a stimulus decrement. Given the same interpretation of x_1, x_2, y_1 and y_2, observe that the concentration in the immediate state does not change when a stimulus decrement occurs. Hence, the decremental response is

$$decrement = kc_1(y_1 - y_2) \tag{22}$$

Comparing this with the 'onset decremental response', which is $k(y_1 - y_2)$, it may be seen that the decremental response does depend on the pedestal level, as reported in the physiological literature [166].

Initial conditions. The initial concentration in the immediate state should be sufficient to produce a spontaneous discharge rate. Letting 'spont' be the normalised spontaneous rate, we have

---

†. The expression for concentration change assumes that the concentration in the relax or reserve state is equal to unity prior to the increment, which it will be if the adaptation to the previous stimulus is complete - this being the usual assumption [166].

rate-intensity functions (model)

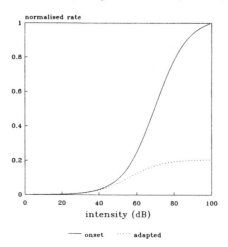

onset   ⋯⋯ adapted

incremental/decremental responses (model)

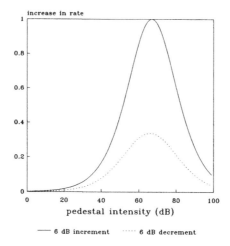

6 dB increment   ⋯⋯ 6 dB decrement

Figure 2.4 *Upper panel*: Model rate-intensity functions at the onset (solid line) and after the response has adapted (dotted line). The y axis is the normalised output minus the spontaneous rate. *Lower panel*: Model incremental and decremental responses. The solid curve shows the change in rate produced by a 6 dB increment as a function of stimulus intensity prior to increment, whilst the dotted curve denotes the rate change produced by a stimulus decrement of 6 dB.

$$c_{imm}(0) = \frac{l}{k \cdot \text{spont} + l} \tag{23}$$

Choice of Model Parameters

With the exception of the parameter x governing the shape of the Crawford and Fettiplace hair cell static nonlinearity, the transduction model requires the determination of just two parameters, the immediate store release fraction, k, and the replenishment fraction, l. This section describes how values for these may be chosen. First, it helps to state some properties of real fibre responses which we may endeavour to match.

Ratio of onset to adapted rate. Some modellers assume that the ratio is a constant (independent of intensity), having a value around 2.5 [166], whilst fibres showing 'sloping saturation' contradict this assumption [167]. Certainly, the Smith and Brachman model, for which this ratio is a positively accelerated function of intensity, is claimed to provide a good match to nerve data. The ratio of onset to adapted rate in this model may be calculated as:

$$\frac{kx+l}{l} \tag{24}$$

which is positively accelerated with intensity. One possibility, then, for constraining parameters k or l is to select a point on neural onset/adapted rate data for some value of x.

Adaptation time constant. As mentioned above, it is possible to compute the time for the system to decay to half the onset response as a function of stimulus level x, k, and l. There is some debate about the value this should take, (and indeed whether or not 2 time constants are required [120],[186]); various values in the range 40-310 ms have been chosen [144], [119], [121]. Clearly, there is some flexibility for matching here.

Recovery time constant. Likewise, it is not possible to provide a single measure of the recovery time constant. Values between 100ms and 0.5 s have been reported.

Given these criteria, the solution adopted was to use the first property, that of onset to adapted ratio, so constrain the choice of k and l for a given x, then select k and l to provide adaptation and recovery time constants in the acceptable ranges above.

In this regard, it is of interest to note that the ratio of onset to adapted rate is exactly (for the model) the inverse of the ratio of adapted to recovery time constants. Hence, for an onset to adapted ratio of around 2.5 [166], and a figure of around 40 ms for short-term adaptation time constant, the recovery time is 100 ms, which is within the reported range.

Summary of properties and limitations of the hair-cell model

The hair-cell model described above is capable of reproducing the following effects:
- spontaneous output rate with zero level stimulus;
- short-term adaptation, with a time constant of 40 ms;
- recovery to spontaneous level following adaptation with a time constant of 100 ms;
- additive behaviour in response to stimulus increments;
- non-additive behaviour in response to stimulus decrements;
- onset rate-intensity function which exhibits sloping saturation at high intensities;
- adapted rate-intensity function which saturates at a much lower level than that of the onset, and has a narrower dynamic range of 30-40 dB; and
- a ratio of onset to adapted rate which is an accelerated function of stimulus intensity, with a value of 2.5 at a stimulus level of 60 dB.

Limitations

The fine temporal structure of the response as measured by a period histogram [143] is not produced by the model. The model was designed to work with the *envelope* of the stimulus, as opposed to the fine time response. This leads to a computationally efficient model which includes additive effects. The pragmatic reason for using envelope responses is that there is no evidence that temporal details preserved in auditory-nerve responses are any more accurate in determining the stimulus frequency distribution than the pattern of basilar membrane displacement with time. Rather, it is likely that the latter is a more appropriate stage at which a model (but not the auditory system itself) could determine stimulus synchrony.

An omission is the rapid adaptation of firing rate with a time constant of a few milliseconds. The analysis of a single reservoir replenishment strategy presented earlier demonstrates that the model is limited to a single time constant of adaptation. It would be possible to produce a two-component adaptation process by including a second source of transmitter replacement in series with the first, as used by Smith and Brachman [168], or indeed, use a three stage process such as that of Ross [144] which would allow for the hypothesised long-term adaptation [99]. This course was rejected for the present model for three reasons. First, there is some debate about the nature of the two-component adaptation effect itself (Yates [185][186]; Meddis [119]). Second, there is disagreement over where to locate the cause of rapid adaptation. Some authors claim that it is primarily a refractory effect (Johnson and Swami [93]), whilst others (e.g. Westerman and Smith [180]) suggest that it is presynaptic in origin. Finally, it is difficult to derive the relevant parameters for a two-component model by mathematical analysis, as was possible for the simpler model presented here. The alternative is to estimate parameters by evaluating the model using a metric which takes into account all desired response characteristics, a methodology adopted by Meddis [121]. Realistically, such an approach is unlikely to find a set of parameter values which match all desired characteristics exactly, which then leaves the problem of determining which of the model responses is most important to model accurately. In the absence of any physiological guidelines as to appropriate weights, such an exercise will always be *ad hoc* and unsatisfactory.

Hewitt and Meddis [82] provides a recent comprehensive review of 8 hair cell models with respect to some of the criteria discussed above.

2.5 The central auditory system

One theme of this thesis is that psychoacoustics provides (currently) the best guiding principles for making use of the representations provided by a model of the auditory periphery. The present section reviews the post-peripheral auditory system in order to show that physiologically-inspired modelling beyond the periphery is beset by problems.

The discussion of the central auditory system which follows is biased towards work which attempts to explain the functional significance both of the anatomical layout of nuclei and pathways, and of the various neuronal response types. More detailed reviews of the anatomy and function of these regions can be found in Moore [127], Aitkin [3], Irvine [91] and Hackney [81].

Auditory anatomy

Between the cochlea and the auditory cortex lie a number of brain stem nuclei, connected by several parallel auditory pathways. This neural 'road map' is complex and involves both ascending (afferent) paths and descending (efferent) routes. This organisation is reflected on both the left and right sides of the brainstem; bilateral pathways link one to the other.

The first area reached by the auditory nerve after its origination in the organ of Corti is the *cochlear nucleus*. This region is subdivided into the dorsal, posteroventral and anteroventral cochlear nuclei (DCN, PVCN, AVCN). These nuclei have been studied more extensively than the higher regions, to the extent that a cell morphology has been discovered and correlated with certain response types.

Auditory pathways lead from the cochlear nucleus to the *superior olivary complex*. This receives input from cochlear nuclei on both the left and right side. Progressing upwards, auditory signals pass through the *lateral lemniscus*, which also receives binaural input, and on to the *inferior colliculus*. This region is further divided into a central nucleus and both dorsal and external cortexes. The dorsal cortex appears not to receive input from lower down the auditory pathway, whilst it may be the terminus of fibres descending from the auditory cortex. The external cortex receives input from both auditory and somatosensory pathways. Prior to the cortex itself lies the *medial geniculate body*, which relays its transformed signals on to the auditory cortex.

Responses, maps and function

Response patterns of the auditory nerve have been well documented and modelled for over 20 years. By contrast, no regions of the central auditory system can be described so completely, although there is increasing activity in modelling response types in the cochlear nucleus (e.g. [2]).

Cell response types in the cochlear nucleus have been given functional significance (although no concrete assertions can be made). In a series of studies [18][19], Britt and Starr examined the discharge patterns of cochlear nucleus cells in response to both steady-frequency tone bursts and frequency-modulated tones. They found 4 types of response; *primarylike*, which respond in a similar fashion to the auditory nerve, and which might act as a simple relay; *onset*, which respond to the onset of a tone, then fall silent for the remainder; *buildup*, whose response is initially high, then is suppressed and increases only slowly with time; and *pauser*, which respond after a prolonged latency with respect to the tone onset. A study by Godfrey, Kiang and Norris [72] added a further response type - *extraordinary* - to this list.

Anatomical studies have correlated response types with cell morphology. So, for instance, primarylike responses appear to be generated by spherical bushy cells in the AVCN [48], whilst octopus cells may responsible for onset responses.

What is the function of these cell types? Various roles have been hypothesised. For example, onset cells, when faced with a repetitive stimulus, may respond in a one-to-one fashion so long as the repetition interval is of sufficient duration. Thus, these cells may provide a sharpening of a temporal response useful for estimation of the fundamental frequency (Moller [124]). However, Godfrey et al. [72] puts such speculation into perspective:

> It must be evident that the present data do not justify choosing any particular
> theory concerning the role of the cochlear nucleus in behaviour. The correlation of
> unit types suggests that particular cell groups might perform specific functions.
> However, the functions may not necessarily show simple relationships with
> behaviour at levels such as pitch judgement, loudness discrimination, localisation
> etc. Other approaches should also be examined. For instance, specific cell groups
> could operate as an intrinsic part of the mechanism for a variety of different
> functions. (p. 267)

Although made in 1975, this judgement still carries weight. It is likely that observation of single units will give only a partial and possibly misleading picture of central auditory processing. In general, the further away a unit is from the periphery, the less simple its response to 'standard' stimuli such as tone bursts becomes. However, there may be some merit in attempting to model units of the cochlear nucleus, where response types can be categorised, without specifically attaching functional significance to particular unit types. The model may then suggest ways in which the transformed representation might code some salient aspect of the signal of interest. Such an approach has been taken by Pont and Damper [136] (also see Pont [137]). They modelled the auditory system up to the level of the dorsal cochlear nucleus, specifically modelling various cell types. The model was tested with stimuli which exhibited voice onset time differences, as would cue the voiced/voiceless distinction. Simulation results demonstrated categorical behaviour correlated with the voiced/voiceless distinction. It is claimed that such categorical effects are not observed at the level of the auditory nerve. Further experiments of this form may throw light on other cues thought to be of importance in speech processing. It may be that attention is shifting away from models of the periphery towards to cochlear nucleus as more physiological results become available.

Higher up the auditory system, response types become more complex and it is more difficult to ascribe functional significance to particular cell groups. However, some general notions have been suggested. The superior olivary complex is the first of the brainstem nuclei to receive binaural input; hence it is suspected that early processing of dichotic stimuli to aid in localisation of sound in space takes place in this region. One part of this complex (the lateral superior olive) is responsive mainly to disparities in interaural intensity, whilst the medial superior olive appears sensitive to interaural time differences. It is believed that interaural time differences encode the position of low frequency sounds in mammals, whilst interaural intensity differences perform a similar function for higher frequencies.

Further up the auditory pathway, part of the inferior colliculus seems to be involved in auditory reflexes, such as the startle reflex to loud sounds. No specific functions have been ascribed to higher nuclei or the auditory cortex itself, although it is presumed that the latter is implicated in more complex auditory tasks such as source separation.

A complementary approach to determining the sort of processing which particular auditory centres appear to be involved in is the determination of topographic organisation or maps. It has been known for some time that all auditory brain stem nuclei and the cortex are organised into cochleotopic maps; that is, a spatial layout of cells differing in best frequency (the tonal frequency which produces the largest rate response). More recent investigations (reported in [127]) have led to the discovery of other kinds of map, running orthogonally to the cochleotopic organisation. The relevant maps (summarised from Moore [127] and Hackney [81]) are:

- *cochleotopic*, in all regions, mammals and birds,
- *intensity*, in the bat cortex,
- *best modulation frequency*, in the inferior colliculus of the cat,
- *interaural time difference*, in the medial nucleus of the superior olivary complex of the barn owl, and
- *interaural intensity difference*, in the superior colliculus of the cat, ferret and guinea-pig.

These maps are potentially an extremely important tool in determining relevant auditory representations. For instance, the spatial layout of cells with increasing best modulation frequency could serve as a substrate on which pitch is determined.

In summary, the neuroanatomy of the central auditory system is becoming well mapped out. Cell types in the lowest of the brainstem nuclei, the cochlear nucleus, are similarly well described. The responses of some of these may be modelled, whilst the behaviour of others remains uncertain. Whilst it is not possible to ascribe functional significance to much of the higher auditory system, the existence of auditory maps does indicate the kind of parameters which the auditory system is extracting and organising, although the method of their use in processing complex stimuli is uncertain.

3

Auditory representations

3.1 Introduction

There is little evidence to date that auditory front-ends of the sort described in Chapter 2 will, applied directly to conventional recognition architectures, lead to performance improvements in speech recognisers (Ghitza [70]; Beet [10]; Lyon and Dyer [113]; Blomberg et al. [12]). Beet has pointed out that the representations produced by current models of the auditory periphery are subject to extreme local variability. For example, the resolution of harmonics leads to markedly different representations of the same utterance when produced on different fundamentals. Whilst such aspects of auditory transforms might be seen as the cause of problems for ASR architectures, it is preferable to regard them as the representational substrate on which much of human auditory ability rests. What is required prior to recognition are further transformations which aim to produce robust and computationally usable representations of speech and other sources.

Unfortunately, as will be clear from the discussion of central auditory processing in the previous chapter, it is not possible to state what representations are employed by the auditory system. As Bregman [17] says,

> ... we presuppose that we know what a perceptual unit is. Yet it is far from certain
> that we have anything better than our own intuitions to go on. (p.68)

However, in proposing useful abstractions, we *can* do better than our intuitions. The Marrian, functional, approach to auditory processing forces us to ask the question "what is the task faced by the auditory system, and what aspects of the periphery outputs need to be made explicit to tackle that task?". Since the model aims to use the experimental findings of work in auditory scene analysis, it is appropriate to examine the representational vocabulary of the field. In so doing, we find that descriptions of properties such as spectral frequency, amplitude and frequency modulation, onsets and offsets are prevalent. But properties of *what* - auditory channels or some other abstraction? This issue is at the heart of the approach described here and is addressed below.

The composition of the auditory scene

Most work which aims to take auditory modelling beyond the periphery preserves the frequency-specific channel model (e.g. autocorrelogram). It is often argued (e.g. Meddis [123]) that such a strategy is adopted by the auditory system as evidenced by the tonotopic arrangement within each of the brain-stem nuclei and the cortex itself. However, is it necessary to be so heavily influenced by the physical architecture, since we understand so little of what is actually being computed at each auditory locus?

Further, and in common with virtually all work in ASR, such post-periphery models generally employ a frame-based representation of time. The representation can be described as a series of parameter vectors computed at regular time intervals. How can this time-frequency graticule be related to experimental descriptions in terms of harmonics, onsets and the like? Consider how acoustic sources manifest themselves. They often have precise onsets and offsets, generally contain components which occupy a range of frequencies (e.g. formants), and, moreover, vary continuously in time. In contrast, a frame-based view makes no attempt to show how elements relate to each other across time. Similarly, maintaining an artificial separation across frequency channels ignores the similarity of channel responses caused by single source components.

Marr's approach to vision abandoned the regularity of the bitmap at an early stage in processing; it is possible that freeing ourselves of the time-frequency grid has similar benefits for models of hearing. Indeed, a number of authors have noted the potential benefits of a representation which makes temporal relations explicit (Darwin and Gardner [42]; Seneff [158]; Karjalainen [96]; Weintraub [177]; Riley [142]). Such representations promise to be extremely expressive in computational terms, as Riley demonstrates (p. 111). For example, if we can provide a label for a temporally extensive structure, the result of propagating the constraints implied by that structure is a wholesale labelling of overlapping objects. The use of a formant uniqueness constraint in the work of Green et al. [79] is a practical example of this. However, computational procedures which show how such representations might be extracted from auditory data have not been forthcoming, perhaps with the exception of the 'line-formant' characterisation described by Seneff [158]. Darwin [38] points out that

> The large literature on speech perception has addressed itself to the problem of what source-specific properties are perceptually salient but has almost entirely ignored the problem of how such properties could be extracted from the raw acoustic signal. Yet the problem lies at the very heart of successful speech recognition and has radical theoretical implications. (p. 1636)

Making temporal behaviour explicit demands a solution to the so-called 'auditory temporal correspondence problem' (Weintraub [177]). The term 'temporal correspondence problem' in vision (Duda and Hart [52]) denotes the task of identifying which parts of an image captured at some time instant correspond to parts of an image captured at some later time. In auditory terms, the task translates to that of relating frequency regions across time. Unfortunately, there is little experimental data to suggest an appropriate computational model here, although recent work by Bregman and his colleagues (e.g. [25]) has attempted to elicit principles underlying this early grouping task.

If we are to base early processing on accounts of auditory scene analysis, then we should seek a composition of the scene into time-frequency objects which characterise onsets, offsets and the movement of spectral components in time. The representation should allow further parameters such as amplitude modulation rate to be calculated.

This chapter describes one such 'auditory objects' representation, which is termed 'synchrony strands'. Each strand aims to define the time-frequency behaviour of a single spectral component (e.g. harmonic or speech formant). Additionally, strands describe the local amplitude modulation rate, together with instant-by-instant amplitude fluctuations. Work described elsewhere describes how representations of onsets can be computed (Cooke and Green [30]), but

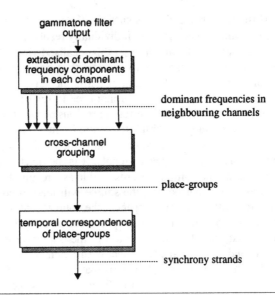

Figure 3.1 Stages in synchrony strand formation.

since these are not currently used in later stages of grouping, their formation is not considered further here.

Section 3.2 explains how synchrony strands are calculated from the outputs of the periphery model described in the previous chapter. One benefit of this abstraction is that it affords a relatively simple resynthesis path, thus allowing an aural evaluation of the information summarised by an arbitrary decomposition into strands. The resynthesis procedure, together with some informal commentary, is discussed in section 3.3. Examples of strand representations of a variety of acoustic sources are provided in section 3.4.

3.2 Computation of synchrony strands

Overview

Figure 3.1 illustrates the processing stages involved in the computation of synchrony strands.

The first stage is *dominant frequency estimation*. The frequency of the most prominent component in the output of each auditory filter is calculated, using median-filtered instantaneous frequency. Estimates of dominant frequency are calculated every millisecond.

Each frame of dominant frequency estimates will contain, in general, a high degree of redundancy caused by large numbers of filters producing similar estimates. The second processing stage attempts to provide a summary of this synchronous activity within a time frame, resulting in a sequence of groups of channels with similar characteristics - *place-groups*.

Finally, place-groups are aggregated over time to produce an explicit time-frequency description of auditory synchrony - *synchrony strands*.

Estimation of dominant components

For a sinusoidal signal, the steady-state temporal response of a linear auditory filter will itself be sinusoidal; hence, it is possible to attribute a known frequency to the response. Natural signals, including speech, consist of a time-varying complex mixture of such components. One of the main functions of the auditory periphery is to separate out individual components. In general, the output of an auditory filter is a combined response to all components with frequencies in its response area. If the filter bandwidth is sufficiently narrow with respect to the separation of components in the stimulus, each may be individually resolved.

There are at least two factors which upset this idealised view of an auditory filter's response pattern. The first concerns the response when more than one component is present in the filter's response area. For example, the interaction of harmonics gives rise to an amplitude-modulated filter response. This effect is particularly pronounced in regions where the filter bandwidth exceeds harmonic separation, but is still present in regions below this, since dominant components are not, in general, exactly aligned with filter centre frequencies.

The second cause of departure from the ideal is the time-varying excitation source, particularly, though not exclusively, for speech signals. It is the quasi-impulsive nature of this source which gives rise to harmonic components resolvable as a result of auditory analysis; however, in addition to the presence of harmonics, the source will lead to correlated time-variation in the output of the auditory filter. In voiced speech, the source consists of a series of glottal pulses. The response of an auditory filter to voiced speech can be considered (approximately) to possess two phases. In the first, the filter output reacts to the impulsive input by approximating its impulse response. Second, if a signal component is sufficiently close to the filter centre frequency, the response of the filter will be pulled towards that component. Responses explainable in terms of this two-phase model can be observed in Figure 3.2(c), which shows the instantaneous frequency of the output of a single auditory channel. Much of the time, the frequency is slowly changing, with a periodic impulse series superimposed upon it.

Collecting these arguments together, it is possible to model the instantaneous response frequency of an auditory filter in terms of a relatively slowly changing component which represents the dominant frequency and a periodic variation correlated with the source. The goal of this stage of processing is to estimate the slowly-changing component. It is possible that the periodic component contains useful information, although it is not utilised in the current algorithm.

The algorithm for determination of the dominant component can be summarised as follows:

1. the *analytic signal* resulting from passing a speech signal through an auditory filter is obtained;
2. the *instantaneous frequency* of the analytic signal is computed;
3. *median smoothing* is applied to the sequence of instantaneous estimates in an attempt to remove variation due to the source; and
4. the resultant signal is *linearly smoothed* to remove any residual short-term oscillation in the dominant frequency estimate.

Instantaneous frequency

The analytic signal corresponding to a real signal s(t) is defined as

$$a(t) = s(t) - iH[s(t)] \qquad (25)$$

where $H[°]$ is the Hilbert transform operator (Bracewell [13]) and i is $\sqrt{-1}$. The Hilbert transform provides a phase-shift of $\pm\pi/2$ to all frequency components, whilst leaving their magnitudes unchanged.

Use of the analytic signal is advantageous in that it provides a variety of well-defined time-domain quantities such as instantaneous amplitude, phase and frequency. An instantaneous frequency parameterisation of speech can be found in the non-auditory work of Seggie [154] and Friedman [62] and in the auditory analyses of Schofield [151] and Beet [10].

The analytic signal is useful in this application since we are interested in estimating an instantaneous measure of frequency (there are other ways to calculate this, as will be shown below). An additional attraction is provided by the form of the gammatone filters used in the

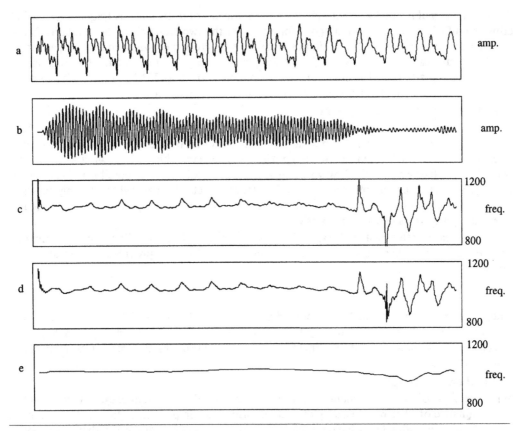

Figure 3.2 Dominant frequency estimation: *a*: waveform for the vowel /ae/; *b*: auditory filter output (CF: 1 kHz); *c*: $v(t)$ by analytic signal method; *d*: instantaneous frequency by linear prediction analysis; *e*: $\hat{v}(t)$.

model's peripheral frequency analysis. The (complex) impulse response of the gammatone filter is given by the expression:

$$g(t) = t^{n-1}e^{-bt}e^{i\omega t} \tag{26}$$

where ω is the radian centre frequency of the filter, and b is the bandwidth.

Under certain conditions (which are very nearly met by the gammatone filter), it is possible to measure instantaneous frequency directly from the filter outputs without computing the Hilbert transform, as the quantity:

$$v(t) = \frac{1}{2\pi}\left(\omega + \frac{\Im(t)\frac{d}{dt}\Re(t) - \Re(t)\frac{d}{dt}\Im(t)}{\Im^2(t) + \Re^2(t)}\right) \tag{27}$$

where $\Re(t)$, $\Im(t)$ represent the outputs of the real and imaginary parts of the gammatone filter. The derivation of this equation is given in Appendix C. Figure 3.2(c) shows the instantaneous frequency, $v(t)$, derived from a gammatone filter centred on 1000 Hz.

In order to validate the method of calculating instantaneous frequency using the analytic signal, an alternative method based on 2-pole LPC analysis was considered. Figure 3.2(d) shows the result of calculating instantaneous frequency using the covariance method[†]. Both LPC and the analytic signal method give extremely similar estimates of instantaneous frequency. Considering the difference in motivation and computation of the two techniques, the similarity is remarkable, but is not pursued further in this study. The conclusion drawn from the comparison is that instantaneous frequency does highlight components present in the signal, rather than introduce processing artefacts. The only other interpretation is that both LPC and the analytic signal method introduce virtually identical artefacts - an unlikely coincidence.

Smoothed instantaneous frequency
An examination of Figure 3.2(c) illustrates some of the features which were noted earlier. The impulsive nature of the periodic time-variation suggests that the trend in $v(t)$ should be extracted using a form of nonlinear smoothing. Here, median smoothing with a window of size M is used, to produce a relatively slowly varying estimate of frequency. It is possible to incorporate a degree of data reduction into this stage of the algorithm. This is achieved by shifting the window within which the median is calculated by Q ms. In the current implementation, the values of M and Q are 10 ms and 1 ms respectively.

In some cases, after median smoothing, there is a small residual oscillation in the estimate. To remove this, a further stage of linear smoothing is applied. This is provided by the leaky integrator:

$$\hat{v}(t) = e^{-kT}\hat{v}(t-1) + \bar{v}(t) \tag{28}$$

where $\bar{v}(t)$ represents the median-smoothed instantaneous frequency and T is the interval between samples at the reduced sampling frequency. This quantity is shown in Figure 3.2(e). The effectiveness of combined median/linear smoothing in estimating the trend in $v(t)$ is clear from this figure.

Calculation of place-groups
Whole sections of the basilar membrane vibrate with near-identical frequency, as evidenced by the dominance of fibre responses by the nearest stimulus component. In the model, instantaneous frequency estimates behave similarly - contiguous sections of the filterbank have synchronised responses. This observation forms the basis for other processing schemes (e.g. the DOMIN algorithm of Carlson and Granstrom [21] and the 'In-Synchrony Bands' spectrum of Ghitza [70]). This redundancy can be exploited to compute a summary of activity across the whole filterbank.

The preceding discussion concerned the value taken by $\hat{v}(t)$ in a *single* channel. Here, we consider it a function of both filter centre frequency and time. Figure 3.3(a) shows the variation of $\hat{v}(t)$ with filter CF in a single time slice t_0. Regions with similar dominant frequency manifest themselves as near-horizontal plateaux (c.f. Figure 5.1(E) of Blomberg et al. [12]).

The goal of this stage of the algorithm is to locate and characterise those intervals along the filterbank which have synchronous activity. The algorithm exploits this *ordering constraint* (note that the use of such a constraint converts what was a place-independent scheme to a place-dependent one):

> A group of fibres with centre frequencies (CFs) centred around a dominant
> component will show an ordered pattern of response; those with CFs *above* the
> dominant component respond with a frequency *below* CF and *vice versa*.

This constraint is illustrated in Figure 3.3(b) which shows the difference between dominant frequency $\hat{v}(t_0,f)$ and filter CF, as a function of filter CF. Zero-crossings in this function corre-

---

†. In order to perform a meaningful comparison with instantaneous frequency, the covariance method was chosen instead of the autocorrelation approach since the former works effectively with small data windows. A window of size 10 samples (at a sampling frequency of 16 kHz) was used in this study.

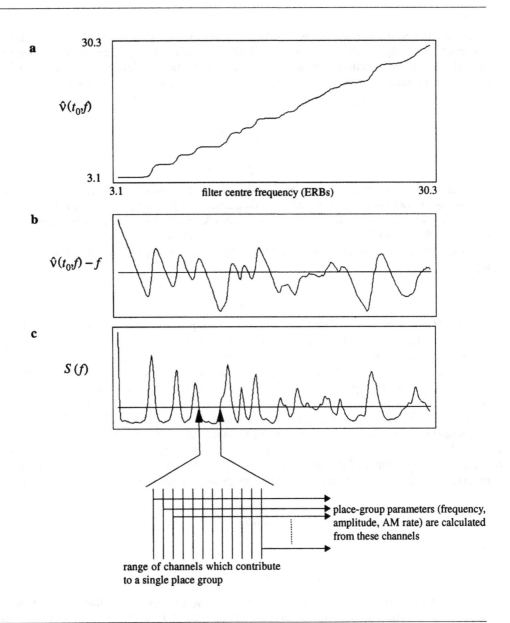

Figure 3.3 Stages in place-group computation.

spond to locations along the filterbank where filters are responding with an estimated frequency close to CF. This can occur for one of two reasons; either a dominant component is located near to filter CF, or the filter is not being drawn to any dominance, possibly because of equal attraction from a pair of surrounding dominances, or else due to an absence of stimulus components in the filter's response area. A consideration of the *sign* of the derivative of $\hat{v}(t_0,f) - f$ allows these two cases to be discriminated. A negative-going zero-crossing in $\hat{v}(t_0,f) - f$ corresponds to the first case.

Rather than identify zero-crossings in $\hat{v}(t_0,f) - f$, we can provide a more robust[†] indication of dominant frequency by grouping together all channels which lie between successive maxima and minima of this function. Formally, for each time frame, we define a sequence of *place-groups* $\{p_i\}$, each corresponding to a range of channels with centre frequencies in the interval $[f_i, f_{i+1}]$ such that the following relations hold:

$$\left.\frac{\partial E}{\partial f}\right|_{f = f_i, f_{i+1}} = 0, \left.\frac{\partial^2 E}{\partial f}\right|_{f = f_i} < 0, \left.\frac{\partial^2 E}{\partial f}\right|_{f = f_{i+1}} > 0 \tag{29}$$

$$\text{where } E = E(t_0,f) = \hat{v}(t_0,f) - f \tag{30}$$

Since $\hat{v}(t_0,f)$ is actually a sampled quantity in both time and frequency, calculation of derivatives is ill-posed (Poggio et al. [135]). To regularise the problem, $E(t_0,f)$ can be smoothed with a Gaussian in f. In practice, smoothing and differentiation can be accomplished in a single step, through convolution with the first derivative of a Gaussian. Hence, a place-group is defined by measurements taken over the interval defined by successive negative and positive zero-crossings of (31), defined as:

$$S(f) = \frac{\partial G}{\partial f} \bullet E \tag{31}$$

where $G(f) = e^{-\frac{f^2}{2\sigma^2}}$ and $\bullet$ denotes convolution. This quantity is depicted in Figure 3.3(c).

The final step is to calculate a number of quantities to associate with each place-group. Specifically, frequency, dominance, amplitude and amplitude modulation rate are estimated.

Frequency. There are a number of ways to estimate the dominant frequency. One method is to use the estimate in channels corresponding to minima of $S(f)$. One problem with this approach is the reliability with which such minima can be located. Further, there may be more than one minimum for each place group (e.g. see Figure 3.3(c)). This problem can be avoided if all channels making up the place group are allowed to contribute to an estimate of frequency. Since some channels provide estimates which are better than others (since they lie closer to the dominance), some weighting of channel estimates is desirable. The quantity $-S(f)$ provides an appropriate weighting. Place-group frequency is computed as the quantity:

$$\frac{\sum_{f_i}^{f_{i+1}} \hat{v}(t_0,f) S(f)}{\sum_{f_i}^{f_{i+1}} S(f)} \tag{32}$$

Place-group frequencies across an utterance are shown in Figure 3.4. Clear representation of harmonic peaks and formant related structure can be seen in, respectively, the lower and upper regions. Similarly, the strong temporal continuity of such estimates can be seen.

---

†. The origins of this decision may be of some interest. Initially, linear rather than median smoothing was used to estimate dominant frequencies. Such estimates were heavily influenced by the *polarity* of the periodic impulse-like structure of the unsmoothed instantaneous frequency. A change in polarity of such features can be observed in the region of a formant (especially F1). This is presumably due to the fact that a 180 degree phase shift occurs across a formant, as noted, for example, by Darwin and Gardner [40] and by Traunmuller [172]. The effect of this on a linear smoothing algorithm is to produce systematic under-estimates of dominant components on one side of a formant, and over-estimates on the other. This in turn leads to the counter-intuitive observation of a pattern of responses in which all filters in a region dominated by some component show responses above CF, thereby contradicting the ordering constraint stated above. For this reason, the more sophisticated estimation technique involving extrema in $\hat{v}(t_0,f) - f$ was employed.

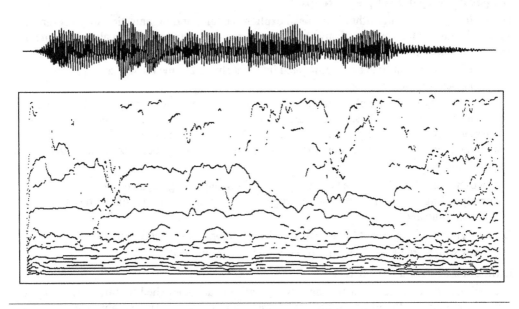

Figure 3.4 Place-groups for the utterance whose waveform is shown. Frequency axis is linear in Hz.

Dominance. Dominance describes the approximate range of influence of a place-group, and is used in later grouping processes. The degree of dominance of each place-group is identified with the spatial extent of the group i.e. $f_{i+1} - f_i$.

Amplitude. An amplitude measure for each place group is calculated by summing the amplitudes of all filters making up the place group.

Amplitude modulation rate. Amplitude modulation (AM) rate is used later in the model for grouping. AM rate is calculated in each filter channel starting from the instantaneous amplitude at the output of the complex gammatone filter:

$$e(t) = \sqrt{\Re^2(t) + \Im^2(t)} \tag{33}$$

The simplest mechanism for extraction of AM rate from this quantity is to measure intervals between successive peaks. Like most feature extraction problems, it is not so simple in practice to obtain reliable AM estimates, since it is not always easy to locate peaks; furthermore, secondary peaks will generate spurious estimates of AM rate. To partially work around these problems, the procedure used here was to first pass $e(t)$ through a bandpass filter (4th order Butterworth, with low and high frequency 3-dB cutoffs of 50 and 400 Hz respectively), then calculate the times of negative-going zero-crossings of the resulting signal. AM rate is then the reciprocal of the interval between successive zero-crossings. Bandpass filtering achieves two things. First, it approximately differentiates the signal, thereby turning the troublesome problem of peak detection (consider broad peaks with shoulders) into the simpler task of zero-crossing location. Second, by bandpass filtering in the range 50-400 Hz (roughly where we might expect pitch related AM), peaks occurring at a faster rate than this are suppressed. Having derived channel based AM rates, an estimate for each place-group is computed using a weighted mean, using the same calculation as in the estimation of frequency (32).

Temporal aggregation of place-groups

The final stage of the algorithm is to make explicit the temporal organisation of place-groups. To achieve this, in the absence of any strong psychophysical data to guide an algorithm, the following *trajectory* principle is used:

> Place-groups at time t are aggregated into that strand at time t-1 whose trajectory passes sufficiently close.

In order to apply this principle, estimates of strand frequency and its derivative are required[†]. Assuming for now that such derivatives are available, each strand is able to predict a location in frequency where aggregable place-groups ought to be found. In practice, a region of size δ centred on the predicted location is computed. Aggregation of place-groups into strands then takes place as follows:

1. place-groups which fall into any of the predicted regions are aggregated into the corresponding strand. It is possible that regions overlap, in which case one of the strands will be terminated;
2. place-groups which do not fall into any such region form new strands; and
3. strands which are unable to recruit place-groups are terminated.

Estimation of strand parameters

The estimation of strand frequency and its derivative is accomplished by fitting the weighted least-squares line to the place-groups which make up the strand. The weighted least-squares line, $y = at + b$ through a series of points $\{t_i, y_i\}$ with weights $\{w_i\}$ is given by the formulae:

$$b = \frac{N\sum_i w_i \sum_i w_i t_i y_i - \sum_i w_i t_i \sum_i w_i y_i}{N\sum_i w_i t_i^2 - (\sum_i w_i t_i)^2} \tag{34}$$

$$a = \frac{1}{N}(\sum_i w_i y_i - b\sum_i w_i t_i) \tag{35}$$

where $N = \sum_i w_i$.

Weights are provided by the dominance estimate in each place-group. However, if such a best-fitting line is calculated using all the place-groups which make up a strand, predictions will progressively become disproportionately dominated by temporally distant place-groups. Hence, instead, a *recency-weighted* best-fit process is adopted. This gives greater weight to estimates which are close to the current 'aggregation boundary'. This is implemented by forming a 'lossy' version of each of the summations above. Instead of using updating formulae of the form

$$\sum_n w_i = \sum_{n-1} w_i + w_n \tag{36}$$

we calculate instead the following:

$$\sum_n w_i = e^{-lT}\sum_{n-1} w_i + w_n \tag{37}$$

Synchrony strand displays are shown in section 3.4.

---

†. The idea of a trajectory principle comes from the work of Ciocca and Bregman [25]. In fact, they suggested that the auditory system might use either a trajectory or a proximity principle to achieve temporal grouping. If the latter is used, derivatives are not required.

Role of each free parameter in the model

There are few experimental results to constrain the parameters. However, it is important to enumerate, and explain the function of, each and every free parameter in the algorithm. Parameter values have been chosen according to the following heuristics:

1. The parameter setting should be robust; the quality of resynthesised speech should not deteriorate markedly when the parameter value is modified within some region around its final setting.

2. If a range of values leads to little difference in resynthesis quality, a value which yields maximum 'computational advantage' is selected. 'Computational advantage' is determined by a number of factors, the most important being computational expressiveness of the representation. For example, if long strands can be extracted using one setting and short strands using another, then the former is chosen.

3. If computational expressiveness is not an issue, then some consideration can be given to computational expense.

Table 3.1: Parameter settings

expression	value
filter spacing	0.3 ERB
M	10 ms
Q	1 ms
kT	0.2
σ	0.4 ERB
δ	0.2 ERB
lT	0.1

The following parameters are free in the model:

Filter spacing. This refers to the spacing of filters in the peripheral filterbank. Values between 0.3 and 0.13 ERB have been used (corresponding roughly to 100 and 250 filters equally spaced in ERB-rate in the range 50-6500 Hz. No significant improvement is found by using the greater number of filters. Computational expediency dictates use of the smaller value.

Median filter window size, M. This parameter is perhaps the only one whose setting is speech-specific. The median window should be large enough to remove the impulsive features present in $v(t)$. An informal analysis suggests that, for a lowest fundamental of 50 Hz, and an impulsive:non-impulsive ratio of 1:1, a window of around 10 ms is required. Other values have been used. Smaller windows produce noisier, but slightly more natural sounding, resynthesised speech, whilst values larger than 10 ms make little difference. Computationally, the size of the median window affects the amount of processing quite considerably.

Temporal quantisation, Q. The value of Q is currently set at 1 ms, which is somewhat greater than the sampling interval of 0.0625 ms, but smaller than most frame-based analysis methods. There seems little point in using a smaller window, due to the effect of median smoothing, whilst significantly larger windows will increase the chance of strand-tracking errors.

Post-median smoothing factor, k, in (28). A light amount of linear smoothing to follow median smoothing is achieved through the use of an exponentially weighted leaky integrator. The time constant of decay for the value of k chosen is of the order of 5 ms. Much larger values would result in a loss of temporal resolution. The exact setting of this value is not critical.

Standard deviation of Gaussian, σ. A Gaussian is used to facilitate differentiation of discrete data. The value of sigma affects the resolution of place-groups. Since this is largely determined by peripheral frequency selectivity, setting σ to a value less than the required peripheral selectivity should not affect the determination of place-groups. Informal listening tests bear this out.

Extent of aggregation region, δ. The value of delta dictates the strictness of the prediction in the strand aggregation process. Small values of δ will result in many small strands, whilst larger values may lead to larger strands, but more tracking errors. A setting of 0.2 ERB was arrived at by inspection of the process operating on a single utterance.

Recency-weighting factor, l, in (37). This loosely determines the time interval over which place-group estimates contribute to linear characterisation. In fact, since recency-weighting is implemented using a leaky integration technique, the parameter is related to the decay time of the exponential weighting provided by leaky integration. The current value was set by visual inspection, and corresponds to a decay time of 7 ms. The setting of this value is not critical.

3.3 Validation of the representation by resynthesis

Motivation

How successfully does the synchrony strand representation model the input signal? A number of researchers have used the methodology of resynthesis as an informal validation technique (e.g. Lienard [109]). Resynthesis allows rapid assimilation of information when compared with visual inspection or recognition tests. Further, signal qualities such as (for speech) gross categories, prosody and speaker characteristics can be determined. An additional attraction for the type of work described here is the ability to continue resynthesis through later stages of grouping, i.e. to listen to the results of grouping. However, it is important to recognise possible pitfalls in validation-by-resynthesis. First, the auditory system may either smooth over or magnify certain representational errors such as broken or incomplete formant tracks. Second, the model may enhance certain features, leading to an unnatural sounding result. Finally, if the model contains nonlinearities, the signal will be subjected to them twice, once by the model, then by the listener, assuming they have the same auditory locus. An example might be an enhancement of onsets relatively to steady-states. So, whilst resynthesis is a valuable method to guide research, it does not measure directly the computational power or completeness of a representation. Resynthesis from auditory representations has been investigated by Hukin and Damper [89] and Ghitza [69]. Also of interest is the work of Heinbach, cited by Terhardt [171].

Resynthesis procedure

Most resynthesis schemes are frame-based. In general, some form of excitation profile is converted to a time-domain signal by inverse Fourier transformation. The method employed here exploits the fact that temporal relations have been made explicit in strand formation. Essentially, each strand is resynthesised as a time-varying sinusoid, with instantaneous frequency determined by linear interpolation of frequency values along the strand. The overall resynthesised waveform is formed by summation of individual waveforms. The method is similar to that used by Quatieri and McAulay [139]. All component waveforms are synthesised in sine phase, with linear onset/offset ramps of 5 ms duration. Currently, no attempt is made to correct for the differing phase delays induced by auditory filterbank analysis.

Initial attempts at resynthesis employed the dominance estimate along each strand as the basis for an amplitude measure. However, a significant improvement in quality[†] was obtained by calculating an amplitude estimate by summing the amplitude measured at the output of the fil-

---

†. A similar judgement was made by Ghitza [69] in his work on resynthesis. He reported an improvement over the use of a dominance measure by using the analysis to select those parts of the original spectrum to be resynthesised.

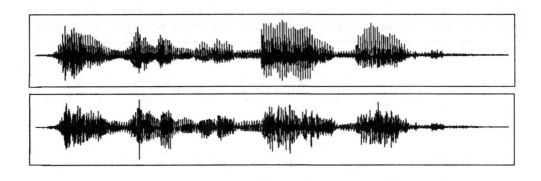

Figure 3.5 *Top*: Original waveform for the utterance "I'll willingly marry Marilyn". *Bottom*: Resynthesised waveform.

ters contributing to each place-group. Figure 3.5 shows the original and resynthesised waveforms for the utterance "I'll willingly marry Marilyn".

Informal listening results

Various signals have been resynthesised using this procedure, including; male/female speech from a variety of dialect regions in the TIMIT database (Garofolo and Pallett [67]); male speech from two speakers in the Edinburgh CSTR speech corpus (Goldsmith [74]); male/female speech from the Leeds database (Goldsmith [74]); locally generated whispered speech and speech with added noise; and synthetic speech from the Klatt synthesiser [101].

It is difficult to describe precisely the quality of the resynthesised signal in a written document. Informally, the resynthesised speech is of very high quality. At best, resynthesised tokens are indistinguishable from the original speech, whilst the lowest quality exemplars remain completely intelligible. This is true across all conditions tested so far (i.e. database, sex, voicing).

In order to push the system to its limits, two more complex tokens were analysed and resynthesised. The first, a double vowel, was used with the aim of determining whether strands might form a suitable basis for work on the separation of concurrent vowels. The resynthesised pair sounded very similar to the original; however, a slight change in prominence could be heard. The second stimulus was a fragment of the 1st Movement of Beethoven's 3rd Symphony, synthesised as a tentative test of the speech-specificity of the algorithm. This fragment produced a greater degradation in quality on resynthesis than any of the speech fragments. Informally, the resynthesised passage might be compared with the type of underwater speech used in cartoons. This might be due to the crude characterisation of attack/decay along the strands. Since amplitude is quantised at the same (1 ms) rate as frequency, there is limited scope for representation of fine structure in the stimulus envelope. An alternative explanation might implicate the existence or size of the median smoothing window.

3.4 A variety of synchrony strand displays

This section contains a number of synchrony strand representations of speech and other sources. In all displays, the frequency axis is linear in Hz (although the analysis takes place on an ERB-rate scale) and extends to 5 kHz. The female (Figure 3.6) and male (Figure 3.7) speech show clear representations of harmonics and formants. Also visible is significant amplitude modulation, particularly in the male speech formants. The regular spectral structure present in the noise burst series (Figure 3.8) is an artefact of the place-group formation process when the input signal is exactly zero. Music (Figure 3.9) shows a complex strand representation, whilst the telephone (Figure 3.10) has the regularities which are expected from an artificial signal. Interestingly, this telephone signature has energy in regions corresponding to speech formants.

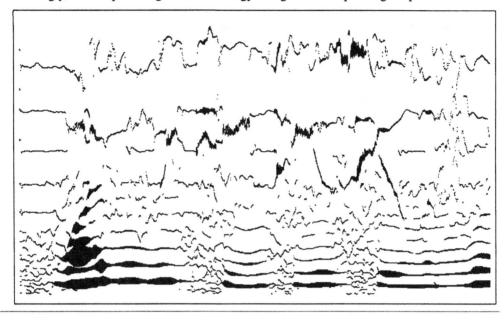

Figure 3.6 Female speech (1.83 s duration).

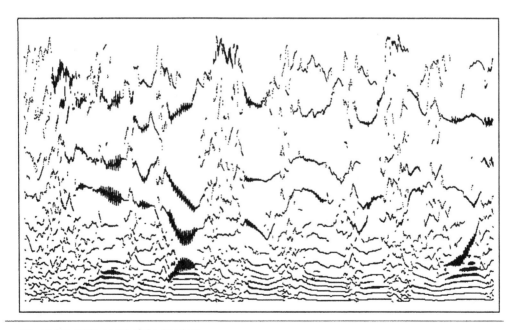

Figure 3.7 Male speech (2.5 s duration).

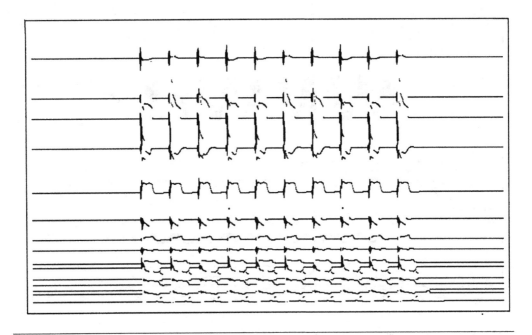

Figure 3.8 Noise burst sequence (1.76 s duration).

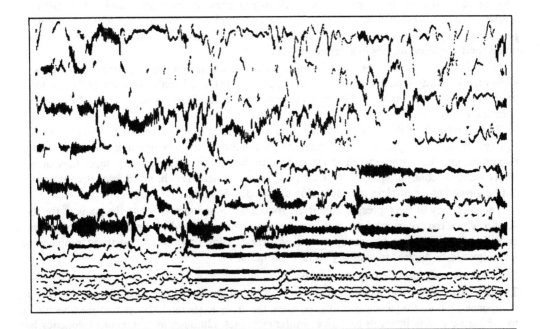

Figure 3.9 New wave music (2 s duration).

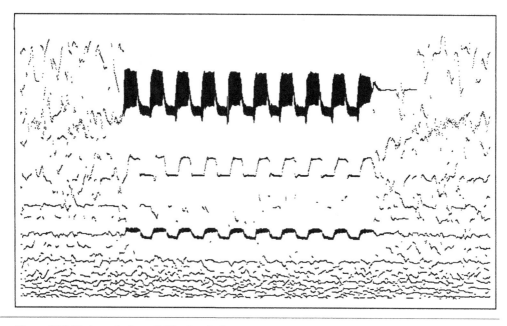

Figure 3.10 Modern telephone (1.83 s duration).

3.5 Discussion

This chapter has described a new auditory time-frequency representation which aims to sum-marise most of the synchronous activity amongst data emanating from a model of the auditory periphery. It appears from informal listening that this information is sufficient to represent both voiced and unvoiced sounds in a variety of conditions.

How should the work be assessed? It is important to consider separately the processing model and the resulting representation. Following Marr [118], the latter is an attempt to provide a partial answer to the question: "what is computed by the auditory system?", whilst the former corresponds to "how is the representation computed?".

The stated goal of this work is to make the organisation of synchronous auditory activity in time and frequency explicit. The algorithm employed is of secondary importance. The following two points are made; first, there is no strong claim that any of the processing stages have an auditory locus; second, in spite of the quality of resynthesised speech, synchrony strands should not be viewed as a complete representation of the speech signal.

The adequacy of the representation itself should be judged in relation to the goals of the thesis, for which the criterion of computational expressiveness should be applied. The next chapter describes how the time-frequency nature of strands allows symbolic constraint propagation techniques to be applied in auditory scene exploration.

Limitations and possible improvements

The first processing stage assumes that each channel of the model contains a single dominating component, whose frequency is estimated using the analytic signal. Other possibilities would be to use zero-crossing intervals to derive similar estimates, although instantaneous frequency has the advantage of being continuously available. The assumption that there is a single periodicity in the filter output is certainly an approximation and not necessarily valid for complex signals, especially those consisting of mixtures of several acoustic sources. Other processing schemes such as the autocorrelogram (Slaney and Lyon [165]) effectively measure the strength of many periodicities present in the signal. There are computational problems in maintaining so much information for many processing stages. However, it would be necessary to compare the ability of 'single-dominance' schemes with 'multiple-periodicity' methods on tasks such as double-vowel separation to determine how much extra benefit is provided by the extra information. Autocorrelation is more 'linear' than the process underlying dominant component estimation in strands. It may be possible to use similar techniques in the initial stage of strand formation.

A further consideration is the effect which smoothing of instantaneous frequency estimates has on the model's capacity to employ certain forms of grouping. Smoothing will attenuate frequency modulation (FM) at rates above some figure which depends on the effective time constant of the leaky integrator used. However, whilst common FM applied to all harmonics of one vowel in a mix will certainly increase its prominence in the mixture (McAdams [115]), there is little evidence that common FM has a role in grouping components together (Gardner and Darwin [64]). If it becomes important to preserve such modulation, it would be possible to accomplish this by adapting the strand formation process in the following way. The smoothed estimates would be used to determine place-groups and ultimately strands. However, the actual frequency associated with each place-group would come from the unsmoothed instantaneous frequency measure.

The temporal aggregation stage is of some importance. The auditory correspondence problem is similar to that of formant-tracking, and is therefore subject to the same kind of errors. Whilst the technique of recency-weighted linear fit does appear to improve the tracking of synchronous regions, and as such might be applied to existing formant-trackers, it is acknowledged that tracking errors might occur. It is, in general, quite difficult to recover in a principled fashion from such errors in formant-tracking. However, there are a number of factors which contribute to both minimisation and recovery from errors in strand formation. First, there is no constraint on the number of place-groups in each time frame; the process of determining higher-level structures is a later one. Approaches which assume a fixed number of formants or resonances are not valid for speech. Second, the combination of a fine frame-rate with a high-resolution frequency estimation algorithm leads to fewer problems in tracking rapid transients. The place groups shown in Figure 3.4 demonstrate a high degree of implicit continuity. Finally, the setting of the main parameter involved in strand aggregation, the size of the aggregation region, can effect a trade-off between the average strand size and the number of tracking errors. A strict setting will result in a larger number of small strands, which later grouping processes might re-aggregate. A more relaxed setting will lead to longer strands, but more chance of errors in tracking. Longer strands are more effective for constraint propagation purposes. More importantly, it may be possible to detect some tracking errors at a later stage of processing, since they will cause conflicting label assignments.

4

Modelling auditory scene exploration

4.1 Introduction

An examination of the synchrony strand displays in chapter 3 reveals a degree of organisation implicit in the auditory scene. Figure 4.1 illustrates some possible groupings present in synchrony strands resulting from the mixture of an utterance with a series of noise bursts. The goal of the processes described in this chapter is to make this organisation *explicit* in the form of groups of auditory primitives which can reasonably be assumed to belong together. The focus of the current chapter is to discuss the computational problems faced in the attempt to recover organisation from the scene, and to outline a framework within which specific grouping principles can be modelled. The details of implementation are postponed to Chapter 5, where the experimental evidence for each grouping principle is reviewed.

Section 4.2 describes the grouping problem which the auditory system has to solve. In particular, computational issues such as search space complexity and the optimality of solutions are raised. The two-stage solution adopted in this work is described in sections 4.3 and 4.4. In the first stage, grouping principles are applied independently, whilst the second stage aims to combine such first-level groupings.

4.2 The computational grouping problem faced by the auditory system

Having decomposed the signal reaching the ears into some appropriate collection of representations, the auditory system appears to select subsets of analysed components in such a way that those primitives which fall within the same group obey some organisational principle, and, when considered together, the groupings form a complete and self-consistent explanation of the listener's acoustic environment.

If the initial decomposition has resulted in a set, $C = \{c_1, ..., c_n\}$, of components, the grouping task might be expressed as one which demands that a collection $G = \{g_1, ..., g_m\}$ of groups be discovered, such that,

$$\forall (g \in G) \cdot g \subseteq C. \tag{38}$$

The approach adopted here is to view grouping as a process which builds a hierarchical structure on to set C, as illustrated in Figure 4.1. The resulting representation is a graph whose lowest-level nodes correspond to auditory primitives, whilst intermediate level nodes represent

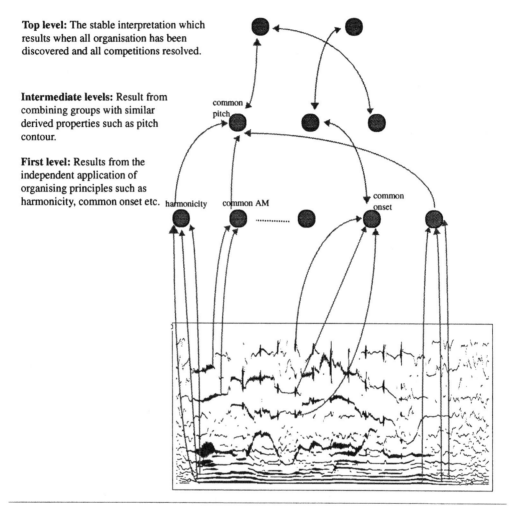

Top level: The stable interpretation which results when all organisation has been discovered and all competitions resolved.

Intermediate levels: Result from combining groups with similar derived properties such as pitch contour.

First level: Results from the independent application of organising principles such as harmonicity, common onset etc.

common pitch

harmonicity   common AM   common onset

Figure 4.1   A hierarchical view of auditory scene analysis.

groups of objects discovered at the preceding level. The upper levels would correspond to more complete *explanations* of each acoustic source - auditory streams. In a full implementation of such a scheme, top-down, or 'schema-driven' processes (Bregman [17]) would be influential as higher levels of structure are elaborated. Here, only bottom-up, or 'primitive' grouping process-es are modelled.

Before describing the model in detail, it is necessary to address some of the built-in assump-tions contained in the problem statement above. Further, since the task is expressed in a declara-tive as opposed to constructive fashion, it is important to consider how the auditory scene may be efficiently searched, and whether it is realistic to aim for optimal solutions.

Computational issues

Divisibility of auditory scene elements

Can it be assumed that the elements of C are not subject to modification by any later process? If the answer is 'yes', then errors made in the formation of auditory primitives may be propagated throughout any further analysis. For example, a synchrony strand contained in C might track first one harmonic, then another. It may be possible to detect this error as a result of grouping. Similar problems could occur at higher levels, after some grouping has been attempted, since objects which do not belong together might be erroneously grouped. The resulting desire to revise the set C, and any levels above, after some grouping has taken place, does not fit cleanly into the model outlined in Figure 4.1, since modifying objects present at any lower level in the graph creates the potential for inconsistencies in already-formed groups at the next level. Similar considerations led to Marr's *principle of least commitment* [117], which suggests that it is preferable to avoid having to undo 'hard-and-fast' decisions made by some earlier process.

For the current application, this principle may be adhered to by favouring tight constraints in deciding which objects belong to a group. This is not a severe limitation, since objects which should belong together have several 'chances' of being grouped as a result of the multi-level representational structure.

Sharing of components across groups

Bregman [17] has suggested a *principle of exclusive allocation* in hearing which suggests that a piece of sensory evidence cannot be allocated to more than one interpretation. For example, this principle would suggest that a harmonic cannot be a member of two harmonic series. Such a principle can be used to describe why it is possible to capture a member of one possible organisation by creating a competing set of components with which it can group (e.g. Bregman and Pinker [14]). Computationally, such a principle would provide a very powerful constraint on allowable collections of groups. In the graph-theoretic terminology used earlier, an exclusive allocation principle would insist that G be a partition[†] of C.

However, there are both experimental and computational objections to an *absolute* statement of this principle in auditory grouping. Bregman devotes a chapter to the theoretical issues surrounding exclusive allocation in auditory scene analysis (Bregman [17], chapter 7).

The assumption that exclusive allocation operates at early stages of auditory grouping is challenged by the existence of so-called *duplex perception* phenomena (Rand [140]; Liberman [108]). Liberman describes an experiment in which a synthetic 3-formant syllable minus the third formant transition is played to one ear, whilst the missing transition is played to the opposite ear. Listeners not only perceive the syllable which would have been heard if all the information had been presented to one ear, but also hear a chirp corresponding to the isolated transition. Thus, the chirp appears to be involved in two auditory streams, giving rise to the term duplex perception.

Bregman's analysis of duplex perception and its antithesis leads him to conclude that the exclusive allocation principle does not apply to primitive scene analysis (those processes which operate on the auditory scene prior to, and independently from, domain-specific knowledge), although if sufficiently strong evidence for allocation of a component can be found, it could be assigned exclusively.

Even if the principle held for primitive scene analysis, there would be computational problems in applying it, centred on the accuracy with which primitives are formed in an auditory model. It is possible that two 'objects' which are separately resolvable in time or frequency by the auditory system may be merged by an inaccurate computer model. Insisting on an exclusive allocation principle might lead to deficiencies in explanation. Whilst every attempt should be made to accurately model the auditory system to avoid resolution errors, it is clear that the computation of abstractions such as synchrony strands can only be partly informed by auditory psychophysics.

---

† A partition of some set is a collection of sets such that each pair of sets is disjoint, and the union of all the sets in the collection is the initial set (C, in the notation here).

A further computational problem in insisting on exclusive allocation is manifest in the search procedure to be described in section 4.3. This algorithm allows similar views of the same group to be constructed from different starting points. Later processes rationalise this redundancy where possible. Such views inevitably share many auditory primitives. Clearly, exclusive allocation has to be suspended to deal with this artefactual situation.

Similarity criteria for group membership

Each group $g \in G$ is formed with respect to some grouping criterion, such as harmonicity. At issue is how well each member of g should satisfy that grouping principle. This is a crucial point for any practical implementation. Where is the line drawn between one element of C belonging to some group and another being rejected? An alternative approach is to rank members of C according to how well they satisfy the grouping hypothesis. Where possible, guidance should be sought from psychophysical studies of the relevant grouping rule. Unfortunately, quantitative data is not available in general. This is an illustration that modelling activity can usefully define appropriate experimental investigations. Some work which proposes to address the problem of providing quantitative descriptions of early auditory grouping processes is described in Williams, Green and Nicolson [182].

Search issues: optimal or just 'good' solutions?

There are many different choices for the collection of groups, G, in the above problem statement, opening up a range of questions familiar to the computer scientist:

 · Is the search strategy admissible[†]?
 · Can an optimality criterion be formulated?
 · How large is the search space?

To these primarily computational concerns, we can ask: how does the auditory system perform this task? These questions are discussed below.

Unlike many problems in speech recognition, it is not at all obvious how to define optimality in auditory scene analysis, which would seem to require an ordering relation between any pair of elements in G. However, it *may* be possible to formulate a criterion by considering some of the properties which this ordering relation could profitably possess. Small collections of groups might be favoured on the basis that it is unlikely that more than a small number of acoustic sources could be present and separately resolvable into auditory streams at any time. A further factor could be the *internal consistency* of groups. Since no collection of primitives will form an ideal group (e.g. precise harmonic relationships; perfect common modulation), some measure of consistency of parts to the whole might be calculated. The total inconsistency of a collection of groups could then be used as the basis for favouring one solution over another.

The problem posed by an insistence on optimal solutions, assuming it is possible to derive a sensible measure of optimality, is the scale of search implied. There are many examples of problems for which there is no algorithm which is guaranteed to find an optimal solution in a reasonable time (this is formalised as polynomial versus non-polynomial time in the computational complexity field [66]). The travelling salesperson problem [103] is often cited as an illustration of this. It is not possible to compute an optimal solution to this problem in polynomial time; however, there are many algorithms which find good solutions quickly (e.g. [97]).

What, then, is the size of the search space for the grouping problem? Consider first the set of all possible *single* groups formed from the components of C. Since each group is a subset of C, the total number corresponds to the number of ways in which subsets can be formed. The set of all subsets is known as the *powerset*, and its size is $2^{|C|}$, where $|C|$ denotes the cardinality of C.

---

†. Admissibility means that the first complete solution returned is guaranteed to be the best.

Identifying the set C with a typical collection of synchrony strands (say, 500 per second of signal), we find there are prohibitively many possible ways in which they may be grouped. Yet the problem is more complex still, since a solution to the grouping problem - a particular value for G - is represented by a *collection* of such groups. It is therefore necessary to calculate the number of ways in which collections of groups can be formed. Again, this is given by the size of the powerset. Hence, the size of the search space is $2^{2^{|C|}}$.

Evidently, it is not practical to carry out an exhaustive search of all possible solution states. It might be possible to reduce the size of the search space by attaching constraints to the optimality criterion. For example, the principle of exclusive allocation might be rigidly applied. Similarly, if some upper bound on the number of groups allowed in a collection were to be used, a further reduction would be possible. However, for reasons outlined earlier, neither constraint is desirable. In any case, such constraints would produce only cosmetic reductions to an unmanageably large search space.

The questions of optimality and search are not often raised in experimental studies of auditory grouping. Instead, descriptions of *strategies* are more common. Such strategies are often presented as heuristics - rules which tend to lead to good solutions. For example, Bregman ([17], p. 349) lists four rules which might govern how the auditory system decides whether a sound has continued through an interruption by another sound. The overriding criterion appears to be simplicity of explanation. The search method employed in this work is based on heuristics, described in section 4.3, which express the belief that it is possible to discover similar groupings from large numbers of different starting points. In practice, the heuristic techniques described can be relied upon to discover most organisation in any auditory scene, partly as a result of the relatively rich decomposition of the signal into time-frequency objects.

A framework for auditory scene exploration

The representational scheme depicted in Figure 4.1 suggests that structure is added to the auditory scene in stages. Initially, auditory objects are composed into groups, then groups are themselves combined. These two processes are treated separately in the model. Section 4.3 deals with mechanisms for producing the first layer of groups, whilst section 4.4 presents a taxonomy of possibilities for combining groups and describes the scope of the current implementation. Both stages employ an identical search strategy, since first-level groups can be considered as elaborate auditory objects.

4.3 Stage 1: The independent application of grouping principles

Much has been written about the way in which specific factors such as onset synchrony or harmonicity constrain our interpretation of the auditory scene. Rather less is known about how grouping principles *interact* in producing a stable explanation of the acoustic evidence. For this reason, the first stage of grouping is restricted to the independent application of grouping principles. The difficult problems in deciding how to interpret the resulting organisation are thus functionally postponed to later processes.

Some of the factors which seem to promote the formation of auditory groups were mentioned in Chapter 1. Recapitulating, components of an auditory scene appear to be perceptually grouped if they are harmonically related, start and end at the same time, share a common rate of amplitude modulation or if they are proximate in time and frequency. There are other factors influencing the integration of auditory primitives, and still others such as common frequency modulation which might appear to be good candidates for grouping principles but which may not be exploited by the auditory system. The system described here allows any of the above to be embedded in a common framework. The experimental evidence for those employed in the current system is reviewed in Chapter 5. The intention in this chapter is to describe the computational framework for auditory scene exploration rather than the details of any specific grouping principle.

Bregman [17] contrasts *simultaneous* and *sequential* grouping. The former refers to rules underlying the cross-spectral organisation of components present at the same time, whilst the latter describes how primitives or groups can be related across time. The first stage of the model might be considered as providing a framework for the implementation of any simultaneous grouping principle such as harmonicity and common modulation. However, there is a sense in which this characterisation is misleading, since the representations in which organisation is sought exist in time and frequency. The temporal correspondence of 'features' has been made explicit (consider the formation of synchrony strands, which loosely employs both simultaneous and sequential principles corresponding to place-group formation and strand aggregation respectively). Hence, any putative grouping of such components by some simultaneity principle such as harmonicity also has an effect on sequential groups, since the two are completely linked in any time-frequency representation. The algorithm described here exploits the power of this constraint in reducing the search complexity.

Heuristics for search

The three heuristics outlined below reveal the motivation for the algorithm which explores the auditory scene.

Explain all the evidence. The search process should terminate when all of the auditory scene has been accounted for, i.e. all objects should be members of some grouping (maybe singleton groups).

Same group, different starting point. Similarity between any pair of objects in a group should be a symmetric[†] relation and, between any three group members, nearly transitive[‡]. This suggests that if the search starts by selecting a 'seed' element, the choice of seed is non-critical. Figure 4.2 shows that, in practice, different seeds can give rise to similar collections of objects.

Start from 'dominant' objects. The more dominant an object is (dominance is roughly correlated with the amount of neural activity assumed to be produced by that object), the less likely it is to represent insignificant or artefactual detail. Similarly, its set of candidate objects for grouping is likely to be large. Hence, search can be more efficient if some proportion of these objects are explained early on in the process.

Putting these considerations together, we define scene exploration here as a process which begins with the selection of the most dominant component, d, in C (dominance was described in chapter 3), then proceeds by seeking to form a group consisting of d and other members of C which lend support to a grouping hypothesis suggested by d. This results in a single group[#]. The process continues with the selection of a new seed as the most dominant ungrouped member of C. Search terminates when all objects in C are explained by some group. This strategy avoids an implementation of the principle of exclusive allocation; groups formed from different seeds may share elements (it is only in the selection of new seeds that previous seeds are excluded).

Constraint propagation

Constraint propagation refers to the way in which groups recruit new members. The current technique exploits the fact that the auditory primitives are time-frequency descriptions in effect-

---

†. A relation is *symmetric* if, for any pair of elements a and b, a is related to b if and only if b is related to a.

‡. A relation is *transitive* if, for any 3 elements a, b and c, if a is related to b and b is related to c, then a is related to c. In the context of a similarity relation between auditory primitives, transitivity cannot be guaranteed absolutely.

#. This is a slightly simplified account. In fact, for grouping by harmonicity, a single seed can generate a number of candidate groups, each based on a different fundamental. The details for harmonicity are described in chapter 5.

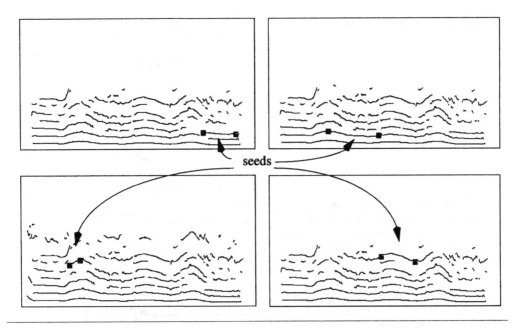

Figure 4.2 Same group, different seeds. This is an example of a harmonically-related group discovered in a natural speech utterance, using techniques to be described in chapter 5. Seeds are the small strands highlighted, each of which is a fragment of a different harmonic (none of which is the fundamental).

ing an efficient search. The method consists of interleaved stages of *simultaneous* and *sequential* propagation, as illustrated in Figure 4.3.

Simultaneous stage. Having selected a seed, the set of strands which overlap with the seed is computed. Such a subset is highlighted in the second panel of Figure 4.3. Each strand in the set is then compared with the seed for similarity. Those which are sufficiently similar are recruited to a group, which also contains the seed. For example, if grouping by common amplitude modulation is sought, then those strands which share a similar rate of modulation in the time region where they overlap with the seed will be placed in the same group.

Sequential stage. Contained within the support set for a group will be elements which start before the seed and/or finish after it. One of these is selected as the new seed (or 'focus') for the group, and a new stage of simultaneous propagation from that strand can commence. In this way, the temporal extent of the group is enlarged, and more of the scene is searched.

Various criteria may be used to select the new focus from a set of candidates:

- choose the strand which provides the *longest extension* to the group;
- select the *most dominant* extension;
- find the strand which is *most similar* to the seed; or
- use the strand which has the *greatest overlap* with the seed.

Further criteria can be suggested by combination of the above, possibly weighted.

Selecting the *longest* extension makes for the most efficient search, but is potentially risky since, if the longest extension should *not* have been part of the group, then the error will be propagated to many other strands. The *most dominant* extension suffers from similar problems, without the benefit of reducing search time. Selection of the strand which is *most similar* to the previous seed appears to be the safest approach, since a high similarity score implies that the

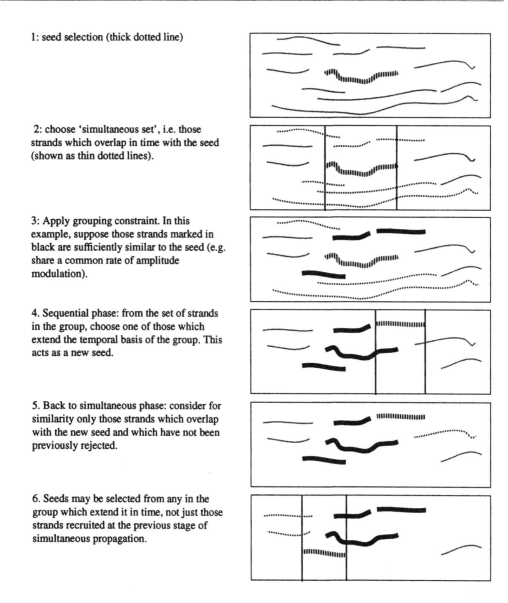

1: seed selection (thick dotted line)

2: choose 'simultaneous set', i.e. those strands which overlap in time with the seed (shown as thin dotted lines).

3: Apply grouping constraint. In this example, suppose those strands marked in black are sufficiently similar to the seed (e.g. share a common rate of amplitude modulation).

4. Sequential phase: from the set of strands in the group, choose one of those which extend the temporal basis of the group. This acts as a new seed.

5. Back to simultaneous phase: consider for similarity only those strands which overlap with the new seed and which have not been previously rejected.

6. Seeds may be selected from any in the group which extend it in time, not just those strands recruited at the previous stage of simultaneous propagation.

Figure 4.3 Scene exploration by alternating simultaneous and sequential constraint propagation.

strand really should be grouped with the seed. However, it is possible for such strands to overlap with the seed by a small amount, so the indication of similarity might be less reliable.

The approach here is to select the most similar extension, so long as it overlaps sufficiently (10 ms is used in the current implementation) with the previous seed. The overriding concern here is to form groups whose members are meant to belong together, even if this means some sacrifice in search efficiency.

Figure 4.4 illustrates how stages of simultaneous and sequential propagation combine to rapidly discover a harmonic group in a set of strands derived from a natural utterance.

Seed (highlighted) attracts several supporters to form a harmonic group.

A new focus is chosen, but recruits few new supporters to group.

New focus (f0 itself) successfully attracts virtually all the harmonically related strands in the utterance.

Process halts when no temporal extension to the group is possible.

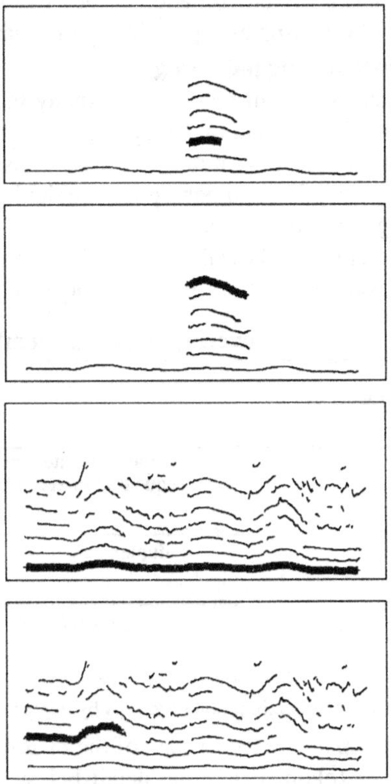

Figure 4.4 Harmonic constraint propagation for a voiced utterance.

4.4 Stage 2: Combining groups

The initial stage of grouping builds the first level of representational structure on to the auditory scene. The second stage aims to determine how any pair of groups formed in stage 1 are related. There are several reasons why it is desirable to integrate groups formed by independent grouping principles. In speech, for example, resolved harmonics grouped by a harmonicity principle should be combined with simultaneous unresolved harmonics in the F2/F3/F4 region which may have been grouped by virtue of a common amplitude modulation. Similarly, harmonic groups separated in time by unvoiced components should be integrated to form a single stream.

There are computational factors here also; the approach to low-level grouping outlined in the previous section can give rise to groups which have many components in common, since it is possible for two views of the same acoustic source to be formed from different seeds. It is natural to attempt to merge such objects, as long as doing so does not result in internal inconsistency in, for example, the estimation of pitch.

The situation is further complicated by the need to allow for duplex perception; that is, it may be wrong to attempt to combine a pair of groups simply because they share some components, since components are allowed to contribute to the explanation of more than one acoustic source. Furthermore, there may be competition for components; some of these result from the algorithms described in the next chapter. For example, in setting up a collection of hypotheses about the fundamental when searching for harmonically-related components, it is likely that several groups will be attempting to explain essentially the same data. Somehow, these competitions have to be 'fought' and resolved. Yet another factor is the increasing influence of what Bregman calls 'schema-driven' grouping as higher-levels of organisation are sought.

A taxonomy for interpreting pairs of groups

From the remarks above, it will be clear that many factors influence the way in which groups might be considered for combination or separation. Some of these factors are related to the algorithmic details of the low-level grouping process, whilst others stem from experimental findings concerning duplex perception and perceptual ambiguity. In an attempt to bring these factors together within a single continuum, consider how the *degree of overlap* between any pair of lower-level groups might indicate how they can be interpreted and assessed for merger or otherwise. Figure 4.5 illustrates these views of group combination.

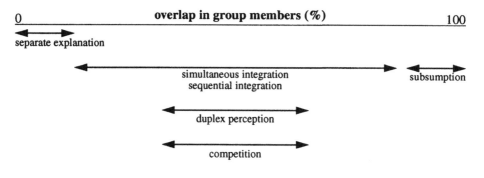

Figure 4.5 Interaction and combination of groups by degree of overlap.

The range of overlap attributed to each of the factors in the diagram is meant to be indicative only. Each factor is explained in some detail below, with particular reference to the way in which it can occur as a result of seeking organisation in natural signals or as an artefact of earlier computational processes.

Separate explanations. If two groups have no elements in common, then it possible that they arise due to two distinct acoustic sources. Each group could then exist as a separate partial explanation for each source. Such groups may or may not overlap in time. To give a rather obvious example, two speakers talking in turn would give rise to such groupings. The separate explanation interpretation of any pairing is shown to range slightly into the non-zero overlap percentage region since it is possible that a small number of components will be shared due to computational inexactness.

Simultaneous integration. In contrast to the above interpretation, groups which have no components in common *may* have arisen from the same source. For example, a group of harmonics may be disjoint from a group of formants occurring simultaneously, yet there could be good reasons for them to be integrated. Such *simultaneous integration* applies not only to pairs of disjoint groups; candidates for merger can come from pairs with quite a lot in common, as indicated by the wide interval in Figure 4.5. The approach adopted in this work to the merger of such groups is based on the similarity of properties derived from each group, explained later in this section. A special case of simultaneous integration is *subsumption*.

Subsumption. At the opposite end of the spectrum, we may find that one group has components which form a subset of those making up some other group. This can arise for several reasons. It is highly likely that the procedure used to generate different estimates of the fundamental will create 'octave error' interpretations (e.g. the series [100,200,300,400,500,600] might give rise to groups [100,200,300,400,500,600], [200,400,600] and [300,600]). Such interpretations can be resolved by applying a simplicity principle, in which descriptions which cover most of the data are preferred. In Figure 4.5, subsumption is indicated to range away from 'perfect' (i.e. 100%) overlap to allow for near-perfect overlap of a pair. Near-perfect overlap might arise when similar groups are built around different seeds. It is a matter of semantics whether such groups are considered as fodder for subsumption or for simultaneous integration.

Sequential integration. Groups separated in time (and thus with no common elements) may belong to the same stream. For example, this situation will arise with any sequence of voiced-unvoiced-voiced speech segments. Merging such groups requires a different approach than that applied in the case of simultaneous organisation. For speech, higher-level factors such as speaker identity (and its continuity), and sentence-level interpretation might be used to determine whether two such groups should be integrated. No sequential integration is currently attempted.

Duplex perception. In contrast to the *separate explanations* interpretation above, this case covers the case when components from two separate acoustic sources are shared across groups. In natural sound environments, this might result from limitations in frequency resolution in the auditory periphery. In the more artificial case of pairs of synthetic vowels on similar fundamentals, it is clear that a number of harmonics will be shared in this way. However, it is unlikely in practice that more than about half of the components will be shared between two objects; this explains the overlap interval in Figure 4.5.

Competition. Finally, there is the case where an overlap of, say, 20-80% reflects a desire by two processes to explain the same acoustic source, and where the two groups cannot be merged or separated by any of the above factors. This may be difficult for an automatic system to deal with, since there is little detailed psychoacoustic guidance on how the auditory system resolves such conflicts in a general setting. That the auditory system has to overcome this problem is clear; indeed, it an inherent part of the experimental technique in this field. For example, in order to assess the strength of some factor in promoting fusion of components, it is often placed in competition with some other known grouping cue (e.g. Bregman and Pinker [14]; Darwin [35]).

Combining groups in the model

The discussion above presents a wide-ranging view of higher-level grouping. The model implements only part of the taxonomy, namely *simultaneous grouping* and *subsumption*. These represent a minimal choice of higher-level grouping processes which still allows for an evaluation of the system's ability to separate speech from a variety of other sources, as described in Chapter 6. Missing from the current system are *sequential integration* and *competition*. *Separate explanation* and *duplex perception* are not explicitly modelled; rather, they represent the default interpretation when other combination processes have done all they can. In other words, the output of the current grouping model is a set of groups, which may or may not share components (the group which accounts for most of the evidence is chosen for evaluation purposes).

Simultaneous integration via derived properties

The basis for simultaneous integration in the model is the comparison of new properties calculated from existing groups. Bregman ([17], p.326) calls these *global properties*. This is in a similar spirit to Marr's aforementioned *principle of explicit naming* ([117], p. 485) which suggests that once a reason has been found for some organisation, an object to represent that organisation is formed (which Marr calls a 'place-token'). Properties of this object are then computed. Here, groups represent organisations of auditory primitives, and candidate properties are *pitch contour*, *energy contour* and *timbre*. In the current implementation the only properties computed are the pitch contour and group dominance (the latter is used in the search algorithm), limiting the application of simultaneous integration to groups where pitch is meaningful (harmonicity and common AM groups). The details of pitch computation are given in chapter 5.

The framework for searching first-level groupings in order to find candidates for simultaneous integration is identical to that adopted in seeking organisation in the primitives themselves. To see why this is so, consider what is required for the search procedure described in section 4.3 to operate. It is necessary to determine seed objects, which requires that all objects have an associated dominance. If objects are groups rather than strands, then the simplest solution is to compute group dominance as the sum of the dominances of its members. The simultaneous and sequential stages of constraint propagation need access to the start and end times of all objects in the scene. Again, it is natural to associate the minimum value of all start times in the group (and similarly for end times) as the start point for the group. Hence, the same search strategy can be used to explore an auditory scene which consists of groups of objects[†].

Reducing the search space via subsumption

In the model, subsumption is an effective way to reduce the amount of search required in finding appropriate combinations of groups. All that is necessary is to calculate the overlap between a pair of groups. If one totally contains the other, the weaker group is removed. The search process starts with the most dominant group, since this is more likely to subsume other groups.

4.5 Discussion

This chapter has provided an account of some of the computational problems in auditory scene analysis and proposed a two-stage framework into which specific principles for organising auditory primitives can be slotted. The implementation of this design is described in the following chapter. The solution to the problem of searching the auditory scene adopted in this work is a heuristic one which exploits the fact that the representational substrate for grouping is a rich, time-frequency description of the signal. The constraint propagation technique can be applied in its current form to any principle of simultaneous organisation. Psychological and computational bases for deciding how pairs of groups should be interpreted, and whether they should be fused or kept apart, have been described.

The architecture defined is designed primarily to accommodate bottom-up, or 'data-driven' exploration, although it is sufficiently flexible to incorporate schema-driven influences. Most importantly, grouping is not attempted in a single step. As a consequence, objects have more than one opportunity to fuse with other groupings. This allows a principle of least commitment to be applied in the form of a strong constraint on which members are allowed to form part of some organisation.

Limitations of the model

The current model does not attempt to perform sequential grouping. However, once pitch contours for groups have been derived, it would be possible to apply continuity constraints to fuse groups which are not too widely separated.

No competition for elements is incorporated at present. Little detailed psychoacoustic investigation has been done in this area, and the experiments which have performed have used stimulus configurations which are too simple to derive general rules for resolving competitions.

Both sequential integration and competition might be expressed in a blackboard computational architecture, similar to that used in the Hearsay-II speech understanding system [56].

One major limitation of the current framework is the 'atomicity of auditory primitives' assumption, discussed in section 4.2. There are situations where it seems necessary to share out the properties associated with a single object between streams. Darwin [38] has shown that if energy is added to a single harmonic in a synthetic vowel, the auditory system segregates some of this energy into a separate stream in order to maintain parsimony of explanation.

---

†. Auditory scene exploration is implemented in CLOS, the Common Lisp Object System. Strands and groups are all specialisations of a class which represents any object which exists in time and frequency and for which a dominance can be computed.

5

Implementation of auditory grouping principles

5.1 Introduction

Chapter 4 defined a strategy for finding organisation in the auditory scene. The computational framework is purposely flexible in that it allows many different sorts of simultaneous organisation to be sought. This chapter describes the specific auditory grouping principles which have been implemented within the common framework. For a number of reasons, grouping by *harmonicity* and *common amplitude modulation* (AM) are chosen as exemplars, although other types of simultaneous organisation such as *common frequency movement* have also been implemented. The choice of harmonicity and common AM is partly due to the strong psychoacoustic evidence for their employment in auditory grouping, a role which is reviewed in the sections which follow. A further consideration is the existence of a common property - the pitch contour - which may be derived from both harmonicity and common AM groupings. This allows the second stage of the grouping model, which involves combining groups, to be illustrated, leading in turn to a minimal system for the separation of speech from other sources, an evaluation of which is presented in chapter 6.

The next 3 sections of this chapter address the first level of the grouping model, in which grouping principles are applied independently. Sections 5.2 and 5.3 review experimental findings concerning the use of harmonicity and common AM as organisational principles, and describe how these are implemented in the model. Section 5.4 describes other potential grouping principles including an implementation of common frequency movement. Later sections present some examples of group combinations and their effect in segregating speech from mixtures.

5.2 Harmonicity

Experimental findings

It has long been known that a harmonic series[†], is not heard as a collection of separate pitches but as a single sound with a pitch corresponding to the fundamental frequency. The auditory system appears to use this cue to group such components together.

---

†. that is, a set of tonal components whose frequencies are integer multiples of some frequency - the fundamental.

One experimental paradigm used to explore the effects of such grouping is mistuning (Moore, Peters and Glasberg [126]). Here, one component of a harmonic series is mistuned so that its frequency is no longer an exact multiple of the fundamental. For small amounts of mistuning (up to 3%), the pitch of the complex changes but the mistuned harmonic makes a full contribution to the perceived pitch. As the degree of mistuning increases, the mistuned harmonic's contribution to the overall pitch decreases steadily until, at around 8%, it has no effect. Beyond 3% mistuning, the mistuned harmonic can be heard out from the rest of the complex.

A mechanism which has been proposed to account for the grouping of resolved harmonics is the harmonic sieve (Duifhuis, Willems and Sluyter [54]; Scheffers [150]). If we imagine a family of harmonic sieves, one for each fundamental, then any member will have slots centred on multiples of the fundamental. The mistuning experiments can be interpreted as defining the size of each slot. However, since the contribution of a partial is not all-or-nothing, a better analogy than a sieve might be a strip of some material whose opacity varied according to the degree to which some component makes a contribution to pitch. In that case, the harmonic positions would pass through all energy at that spectral location, gradually fading to total opacity at +/- 8% from the centre of the transparent region.

Darwin and Gardner [40] explored the effect of harmonic mistuning on phonetic quality using a paradigm involving listeners' sensitivity to F1 frequency in discriminating /I/ and /e/. Exclusion of a harmonic close to the F1 peak has the effect of shifting the phoneme boundary. They demonstrated that mistuning a harmonic in the F1 region of a synthetic vowel can change its phonetic quality in a manner predictable by a harmonic sieve mechanism and have concluded that grouping criteria which operate for pitch may also be implicated in the calculation of F1 frequency for speech.

Implementation

Recall from the previous chapter that auditory scene exploration begins with the selection of strands as seeds. To model the harmonicity grouping principle, it is necessary to interpret a seed as one harmonics of some series. But which harmonic? As an example, a strand whose frequency is 240 Hz might correspond to the fundamental, or the first, second or third harmonic of series with fundamentals of 120, 80 or 60 Hz respectively. Each seed therefore generates a *set* of candidate values for the fundamental. The range of interpretations for a seed can be limited to restrict hypothesised F0's to some defined frequency region. Here, the region is 70-400 Hz. The example presented above is simplified in one respect - strands are not static in frequency, but vary in frequency with time. Hence, it is possible to pose a more restrictive condition on allowable fundamentals which examines the *extrema* in frequency over which the seed ranges. The frequencies at such extrema have to generate F0 hypotheses which lie within the allowed range. For example, a strand which rises from a minimum of 120 Hz to a maximum of 240 Hz will be considered to be either the fundamental, or the first harmonic of a 60 Hz fundamental. This stronger constraint is an example of the way in which a time-frequency representation can limit computation.

Figure 5.1 shows 5 harmonic groups generated in response to a seed strand, which is highlighted in the left panel. The signal is a synthetic harmonic series consisting of equal amplitude tones at 100 Hz and its first 7 harmonics. The five groups represent hypothesised fundamentals of, from the top, 400, 200, 133.3, 100 and 80 Hz, corresponding to the seed (which is at 400 Hz) being considered either as the fundamental, or as H1, H2, H3 or H4 of a harmonic series. Components of the auditory scene on the left which are grouped according to each hypothesis are shown as thick lines in the panels on the right of the figure. Each hypothesis generated in the manner described above defines a harmonic sieve extended over the time interval occupied by

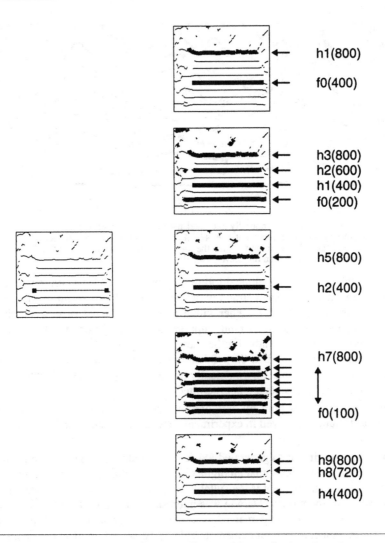

Figure 5.1 An illustration of the harmonic groups discovered in a collection of synchrony strands shown on the left. The seed is highlighted in the left panel.

the hypothesis, as shown in Figure 5.2. It is thus possible to measure how well each component in the auditory scene fits into one of the 'channels' carved out by the sieve over time.

The actual fit is determined by applying the 3-8% contribution function shown in Figure 5.3 to each time frame in the overlap between the hypothesis and tested component, and then normalising by the length of the overlap. For example, if a component falls exactly in the centre of a sieve channel for the whole of its length, it will achieve a perfect score of 1, whilst if it some way from the centre (say, 5% mistuned) for its length, or if it falls completely outside the channel some of the time, it will get a lower score. It is possible that a component might fall into more than one sieve channel, in which case it will obtain a set of fits, one for each channel. The result of this stage of processing is that each component in the scene has a labelling which maps one or more sieve channels to scores in the range 0-1. To complete one phase of simultaneous propagation, it is necessary to decide which strands should form a group with the seed. There

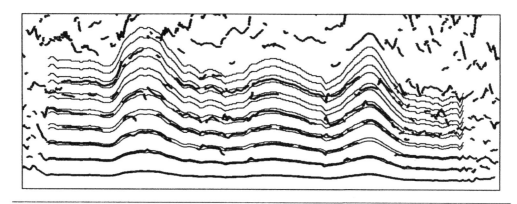

Figure 5.2 One of a series of temporally-extended harmonic sieves generated from a seed strand. Thin lines represent the +/-3% boundaries of sieve channels. Some strands fall wholly or partly into the sieve, whilst others do not. Strands may contribute to more than one sieve channel.

are several possibilities; the one adopted follows the principle of least commitment by requiring good evidence for inclusion. Each strand which is processed as a result of the sieving process will either possess a unique label together with a score for that label, or will contain multiple labels each with an individual score. Strands supporting the hypothesis must be drawn solely from the set of *uniquely labelled* strands. Furthermore, the degree of fit to a sieve channel must be greater than a threshold (set here at 0.8). Taken together, these rules virtually guarantee that all elements of a harmonic group are harmonically related throughout the time interval occupied by the group, even if other elements are not recruited.

In order to illustrate grouping by harmonicity (and, in section 5.3, by common amplitude modulation), a stimulus employed in experimental studies of grouping by a common fundamental was used.

Darwin ([35], experiment 4) generated a 4 formant synthetic syllable with formant contours carefully chosen to create perceptual ambiguity. If the stimulus is synthesised without the fourth formant, the predominant percept is the syllable /ru/, whilst if the second formant is omitted, the main response of listeners is /li/. Darwin was interested in conditions under which the four formants played together could be perceived as either /ru/ or /li/, and showed that, if all formants were synthesised on a common fundamental, /ru/ was perceived on most occasions. However, if the second formant was synthesised on a different F0, the number of /li/ responses increased.

The top panel of Figure 5.4 illustrates the strands produced for a similar stimulus used in a later study by Gardner, Gaskill and Darwin [65]. The syllable has its first, third and fourth formants synthesised on a fundamental of 110 Hz, whilst the second formant is synthesised on a

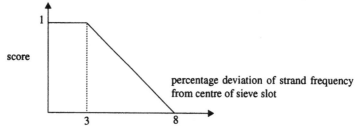

Figure 5.3 The 3-8% scoring function used in assessing how well strands fit sieve slots.

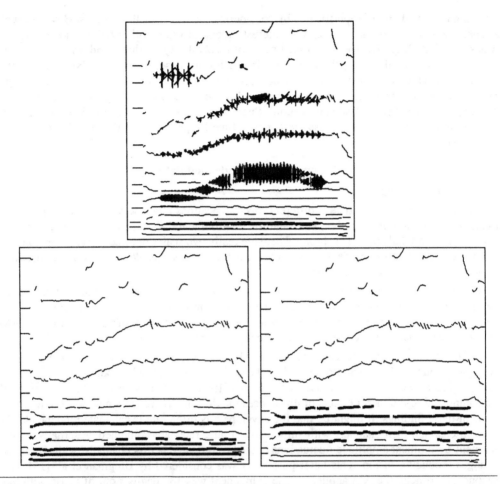

Figure 5.4 Strand analysis and harmonic groups discovered in a synthetic 4-formant syllable (see text for details). Frequency axes are linear in Hz and extend to 5 kHz.

fundamental of 174 Hz. Note that the spacing of harmonics in the F2 region differs from that in the F1 region.

The two main harmonic groups discovered by the algorithm are depicted in the lower part of Figure 5.4. One group consists largely of harmonics of 110 Hz in the region of the first formant, although one harmonic in the second formant region has been recruited, presumably because it falls close to one of the harmonics of 110 Hz. The other group has captured most of the harmonic information in the F2 region. Note that there is some sharing of components across the two organisations. Harmonicity clearly provides a basis for segregating information in the F1 region from that in the F2 region in this example. However, this stimulus is taken from one extreme of a series in which the fundamental on which F2 is produced varies from 2 Hz to 64 Hz. For smaller amounts of 'formant mistuning', harmonics in the F2 region are not resolved.

Discussion

Harmonicity is somewhat exceptional in this framework since it is the only grouping principle for which we have not only a suggested mechanism (the sieve) but also a fairly precise metric for determination of similarity (the 3-8% mistuning function). However, the criterion for inclusion might be made more sophisticated by considering multiply labelled strands. How can such a labelling arise? There are at least two interesting possibilities. Either the harmonic number was sufficiently high that we are on the border of resolvability, or the strand tracked one harmonic for some of the time, then another. In the former case, we might wish to count the 'merged' structure as evidence for the hypothesis if the combined score was sufficiently high. However, the latter case suggests a potential for discovering and correcting an error made in an earlier process (namely, strand aggregation). Such conflict spotting and resolution is not implemented in the current system, but suggests how a time-frequency representation can be used to facilitate explanations.

5.3 Common amplitude modulation

Experimental findings

Correlated changes in amplitude at different spectral locations might serve as a cue for grouping those frequency regions together, since natural environmental signals tend to possess components which start and end in synchrony. There are really two scales of effect here, corresponding to onsets/offsets and amplitude modulations. Here, the latter is considered; the role of onset/offset synchrony is reviewed in section 5.4.

When two or more harmonically-related components fall into the response area of an auditory filter, they are not separately resolved; instead, the output is amplitude modulated at a rate equal to the difference in the harmonic frequencies. Hence, detection of common rates of AM could serve as a factor which helps to bind the higher formants of speech together.

Bregman, Abramson, Doehring and Darwin [15] showed, albeit as a rather weak effect, that two tones tended to fuse most strongly when the same rate of amplitude modulation was applied to them. More recently, Bregman, Levitan and Liao [16] extended this result to larger degrees of mistuning and found larger effects of differences in AM rate. There are a number of interpretations of these findings. It might be that the envelope repetition rate is calculated independently in each channel, then channels with sufficiently similar rates are combined. Alternatively, the moment-by-moment amplitude fluctuations could be compared across channels, with correlated changes producing fusion. This latter possibility was considered by Bregman et al. [15]. In a second experiment, the AM applied to one component was 180 degrees out of phase with that applied to the others. The tones fused less strongly in this case. From this single experiment, it is possible to speculate that fusion of spectral components might be on the basis of correlated, instantaneous changes in amplitude rather than on common AM rate. However, further studies are required to replicate and quantify this effect. There may be two mechanisms at work, one which correlates changes in amplitude, and another which correlates rates of AM. For natural speech sounds, at least for the region occupied by the second and third formants, both common AM rate and correlated cross-spectral changes will generally be present; hence, both will be available to grouping mechanisms to aid in binding speech formants together.

Implementation

It is possible to exploit both potential grouping mechanisms - common envelope repetition rate and common amplitude fluctuations - in the model. Similarity scores between seed and each overlapping strand are calculated using metrics sim_{rate} and sim_{env} defined below. The maximum value of the two metrics is chosen, and a threshold (currently set at 0.8) is applied to this figure to determine those strands which form a group with the seed.

Common envelope repetition rate. Envelope repetition rate is calculated according to the scheme described in chapter 3, and is available at each time point along strands. There are several possibilities for computing the degree of similarity in envelope repetition rate between a pair of strands. The computation used here is the average pointwise similarity in rates. The similarity *sim(x,y)* between a pair of instantaneous AM rates *x* and *y* is calculated using the formula

$$sim\,(x,\,y)\ =\ e^{-\frac{1}{2}(\frac{x-y}{\sigma})^2} \tag{39}$$

where the standard deviation of the Gaussian, σ has the value 25 Hz in this work. In using this form of similarity measure, the assumption is that a small difference in AM rate is tolerated by the auditory system, corresponding to the broad top of the Gaussian. Clearly, the choice of width for this kind of AM sensitivity function is somewhat arbitrary - there is a need for psycho-physical studies to indicate the width and shape of this function. The data produced by recent investigations of the grouping power of AM (e.g. Bregman, Levitan and Liao [16]) are too sparse to be interpreted as a strict metric.

Framewise measures of similarity are summed over the interval corresponding to the overlap between the seed and other strands considered for grouping, and divided by the length of the overlap. If $r_{seed}(t)$, $r_{strand}(t)$ represent the computed amplitude modulation rate as a function of time for the seed and the strand which is being compared for similarity, and if the strands overlap in the time interval $[t_1, t_2]$, then the similarity is computed using:

$$sim_{rate}\ =\ \frac{1}{t_2 - t_1}\sum_{t\,=\,t_1}^{t_2} sim\,(r_{strand}(t),\,r_{seed}(t)) \tag{40}$$

The principal advantage of this metric over, for example, the Euclidean distance, lies in its treatment of gross errors in the measurement of AM rate. The Euclidean distance is heavily influenced by such errors, whilst the similarity metric defined above merely records a near-zero similarity over those frames which have radically different AM rates, thereby tolerating a small number of such 'rogue' points.

Common amplitude fluctuations. Potentially, all synchrony strands will show some amplitude modulation. However, the greatest depth of modulation will occur, for speech at least, in the region where harmonics are unresolved. Modulation depth is related to the relative amplitudes of two or more constituents when filtered, which depends partly on the relationship between harmonic spacing and peripheral frequency resolution, and partly on formant bandwidth. The upper resolved harmonics also possess some amplitude modulation.

Since phase of modulation is critical in this form of comparison, it is necessary to correct for phase delays introduced by the filterbank. Holdsworth et al. [85] describe two forms of phase alignment which may be performed on gammatone filter outputs. The first, based on an alignment of impulse response envelopes, is used here. The starting frequency of each strand is used as the nominal centre frequency of a gammatone filter, and the corresponding phase lag for that filter is computed using (41). This value is subtracted from the start and end times of each strand to effect the phase correction. The formula is obtained by differentiating the lowpass gammatone. The peak of the envelope corresponds to the time of the first zero-crossing of its differential, and is given by:

$$t_{max}\ =\ \frac{n-1}{2\pi b} \tag{41}$$

where *n* is the filter order (equal to 4 here) and *b* is its bandwidth.

In order to obtain an estimate of the similarity in the pattern of amplitude modulation which is not influenced by either depth of modulation or overall amplitude, strand amplitude vectors are normalised by removing the mean and rescaling to produce unity variance. The similarity between a pair of synchrony strands can then be expressed as the cross-correlation between

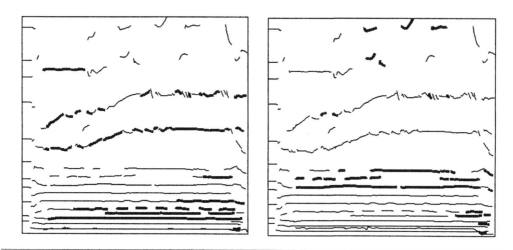

Figure 5.5 Amplitude modulation groups.

these normalised amplitude vectors - a figure which is calculated over the region where the pair overlap. Letting $a_{seed}(t)$, $a_{strand}(t)$ represent the amplitude of seed and strand at time t, then the similarity metric applied to these strands is:

$$sim_{env} = \sum_{t=t_1}^{t_2} \hat{a}_{strand}(t)\,\hat{a}_{seed}(t) \tag{42}$$

where $\hat{a}(t)$ is the normalised amplitude at time t.

The /ru/-/li/ stimulus discussed earlier illustrates grouping by common amplitude modulation. Figure 5.5 shows the principal AM groups discovered in the auditory scene. The left panel shows grouping of information in the F3 and F4 regions, as might be expected. Perhaps the most notable point illustrated by this figure is the inclusion of some of the harmonics of F1, an indication that strands representing harmonics possess some amplitude modulation despite being separably resolvable in the filterbank. The right panel shows a grouping of some harmonics in the F2 region. The difference in AM rates which gives rise to these groupings is visible in the strand analysis of Figure 5.4 (top panel)

There are therefore two bases for the segregation of F2 in this stimulus. Gardner et al. [65] used a series of stimuli with F2 synthesised on 110, 112, 114, 118, 126, 142 and 174 Hz. There will be a point along this series with increasing F2 'fundamental' at which harmonics in the F2 region become resolved for the first time. Prior to this point, grouping may be on the basis of differences in amplitude modulation rate. Interestingly, Gardner et al. noted that listeners report hearing two sources for a smaller F2 'mistuning' than the amount at which they report a change in phonetic percept from /ru/ to /li/. The phonetic judgement might correspond to the point at which harmonics become resolved; at this point, the auditory system has both common AM *and* harmonicity criteria for segregating F2.

5.4 Other principles for simultaneous grouping
Common frequency modulation and movement
As in the case of common amplitude modulation described above, coherent variations in frequency across different spectral regions could serve as a cue that components belong to the same external source. In contrast to common AM, however, experimental support for this factor

is rather weak. It is necessary to distinguish two time scales of common frequency change, namely, fairly small modulations (1-10%) in the fundamental frequency of the sort which accompany sung voiced sounds, or longer-term movement of the fundamental which results in parallel (on a log-scale) movement of all the harmonics of that fundamental.

McAdams [115] has studied the former using harmonic complexes in which one partial was frequency modulated with a different function to that used on the remaining harmonics. In one condition - incoherent modulation - the applied modulation destroyed harmonic relationships. Subjects reported more than one sound source. However, in a different experiment, coherent modulation - preserving harmonic relationships - was applied to each fundamental of a three-vowel mixture. Such modulation made the vowel more prominent, but differences in modulation between vowels did not help in increasing prominence. Gardner and Darwin [64] attempted to find an effect of incoherent FM by modulating one harmonic of a vowel at a different rate from other components. Any exclusion of that component from a group ought to have an effect on the phonetic category reported by listeners. No effect of incoherent FM was found. More recently, Gardner, Gaskill and Darwin [65] sought effects of coherent or incoherent FM in grouping together formants of a 4-formant syllable. Earlier studies by Darwin [35], outlined above, showed clearly that a static difference in the fundamental applied to one of the formants allowed it to be segregated from the remaining formants. However, Gardner et al. found no comparable effect when the equivalent formant was subjected to incoherent or coherent FM. The general conclusion from these studies is that, whilst common FM can influence the number of sources perceived, it has little if any effect on perceptual grouping.

Note that common frequency movement is a necessary, but insufficient, condition for harmonicity. As such, it might be viewed as providing an alternative computational strategy for the computation of harmonically-related groups. In the first stage, components with common frequency movement could be grouped according to a correlation-based algorithm. Then, a check for harmonicity could be made. Apart from possible computational advantages such as rapidity of calculation, this approach has a possible benefit over that outlined in the section on harmonicity above, in that it does not involve hypothesising a fundamental until the second stage. The harmonicity scheme requires that the seed generates a value for the fundamental. Different seeds will generate different fundamentals. It is possible that some of these are less accurate than others, so the harmonic sieve generated will not be as effective in all cases. By avoiding reliance on a calculated fundamental until a second stage of grouping, use of common frequency movement produces groups which are neutral to the choice of seed.

Since common FM is a simultaneous organisational principle (albeit one which appears not to be used in perceptual grouping), it can be implemented within the framework described in chapter 4. In a similar fashion to the process described for common AM, common frequency movement can be detected by cross-correlating appropriately normalised frequency vectors of the seed and each candidate for grouping. Figure 5.6 compares grouping by harmonicity with that by common FM. The signal is a synthetic complex consisting of 5 harmonically-related swept frequency components, together with a mistuned component which maintains a constant, but inharmonic, frequency ratio with the surrounding glides. The strands produced for this signal are shown in the left of Figure 5.6. The top right panel shows the group formed by a common FM principle, whilst the lower right panel results from applying a harmonicity principle. The mistuned component stands out clearly in the harmonicity figure, yet is grouped by common FM, as expected.

It should be noted that the type of common FM detectable here is limited by earlier smoothing processes inherent in the formation of synchrony strands. Since instantaneous frequency estimates are smoothed prior to cross-channel grouping much of the microstructure of frequency

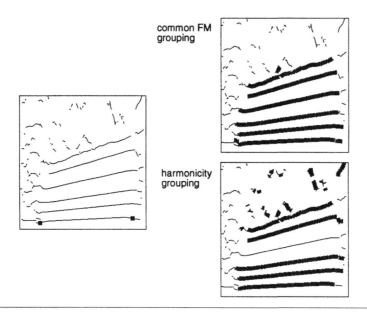

Figure 5.6 An illustration of grouping by common frequency movement. *Left*: strands for a six component signal (see text for details). *Top right*: a common FM group discovered in the scene. *Bottom right*: an organisation resulting from seeking harmonically-related objects.

modulation is lost, although it is possible to reintroduce it if we view smoothing simply as a means of allowing appropriate channels to be grouped.

Onset and offset synchrony

In a natural acoustic environment, sound components arising from the same source tend to start and end synchronously. Can the auditory system make use of this cue in scene analysis? Darwin [35] found a small effect of formant onset asynchrony in promoting fusion between the remaining synchronous formants in the four-formant syllable paradigm described earlier. Using a 300 ms lead on the second formant, listeners were more likely to report /li/ rather than /ru/. Using a different paradigm, the /I/-/e/ boundary shift method also described earlier, Darwin [38] and Darwin and Sutherland [39] showed that a small onset asynchrony (of the order of 20 ms) in a vowel harmonic causes a phoneme boundary shift, suggesting that it makes less of a contribution to vowel quality than if it had started at the same time as the other harmonics. Darwin and Sutherland also found a similar effect for offset asynchrony. Furthermore, they disconfirmed the hypothesis that the effect could be solely due to adaptation in auditory nerve fibre responses rather than perceptual grouping.

No explicit representation of onsets and offsets is reported in this thesis (although some initial work on onset groups is described in Cooke and Green [30]). Onset and offset information is implicit in groupings of synchrony strands, and might be exploitable at a higher level of grouping. Note that onsets and offsets of individual strands are not necessarily related to the appearance and disappearance of acoustic sources. It is more likely that spurious onsets are produced by the strand aggregation process, which would sooner break a strand than risk a tracking error.

Although onset/offset synchrony is an example of simultaneous organisation, it would not be appropriate to use the constraint propagation framework described in chapter 4 to seek such groupings, since the sequential phase might allow a chain of onsets whose total time extent is rather large to be grouped together, as shown below. A simpler scheme which employs a single simultaneous phase might be all that is required.

5.5 Higher-level grouping

Derived properties

Here, the sole derived property is *pitch contour*. Pitch is computed from harmonic groups and from those grouped by common AM, using techniques described below.

Pitch contour calculation from harmonic groups

There are several possibilities for the computation of pitch from a group of harmonically-related components. Since each strand in a harmonic group knows which harmonic it represents, it would be possible to employ some pitch meter which weights harmonics according to the harmonic number (e.g. Goldstein's maximum likelihood estimate [75], or the modification derived by Duifhuis, Willems and Sluyter [54]). One problem of an approach which uses all the grouped components is that we cannot guarantee that each component is present at each time frame in the group. Indeed, it is generally the case that strands representing harmonics exist in fragmented time intervals (see Figure 5.2).

The approach adopted here is to use the estimate of the fundamental generated by successive seeds used to create the harmonic group. The collection of seeds for each group is guaranteed to cover every time frame from the start of the group to its end due to the manner in which sequential constraint propagation is implemented.

Pitch contour calculation from AM groups

The pitch contour for an amplitude modulation group is produced in a similar fashion. The relevant parameter used in this calculation is amplitude modulation rate, even though the grouping may have been produced by common instant-by-instance amplitude modulation. AM group pitch contours are generally less smooth than those derived from harmonic groups. The scheme for computing AM rate described in chapter 3 is rather simple; it may be possible to derive better estimates of envelope repetition rate using autocorrelation, for example. The current emphasis is on showing how it would be possible to use such a parameter for grouping, and there is clearly scope for improvements in the way such features are estimated.

The upper left panel of Figure 5.8 shows the pitch contours derived from all harmonicity and amplitude modulation groups discovered in the /ru/-/li/ stimulus. There are several interesting features of these contours. First, there are clusters of estimates around the 110 Hz and 174 Hz regions, corresponding to some of the groups depicted earlier in the chapter. Combining such groups on the basis of pitch contour similarity is described below. Second, some of the contours are extremely erratic. These are all due to difficulties in estimating amplitude modulation rate. The third feature of this figure is a 'ladder' effect where a single seed has generated a number of estimates for the fundamental, as described in section 5.2 on harmonicity. Some of the groups responsible for these can be removed by the subsumption principle, described below.

Group combination

Of all the principles for combining groups discussed in chapter 4, two are implemented. *Subsumption* seeks to remove groups whose elements are contained in a larger grouping. *Simultaneous integration* attempts to combine groups whose derived properties are sufficiently similar. In the model, this amounts to a comparison of pitch contours.

Subsumption is applied twice in the current model. It is applied both before and after the attempt to fuse groups based on common pitch contour. Since subsumption reduces the size of the search space, it is rational to apply it prior to simultaneous integration. The reason for a second application lies in the observation that the integration of groups may produce collections which are subsets of other groups. Some statistics on the effectiveness of subsumption and simultaneous integration are provided in Table 5.1 below, which is based on an analysis of 100 auditory scenes (precisely those which are used in the evaluation described in chapter 6).

Table 5.1: elements and groups in the auditory scene at various stages in exploration.

object type	mean	sd	min	max
strand	567	212	251	1180
harmonic/AM group before subsumption	66	25	20	140
harmonic/AM group after subsumption	34	15	8	7
combined group before subsumption	26	12	3	60
combined group after subsumption	22	12	2	57

Subsumption

Subsumption is designed to remove those groups whose elements are totally contained within a larger grouping. Ideally, a subset relationship could be used to detect such situations. However, it is likely that groups will be nearly contained within others, but that a small number of elements lie outside the larger organisation. A further consideration is that not all elements are equally dominant in the scene. In order to decide whether a group $g1$ should be subsumed into a group $g2$, the following metric is applied to the groups:

$$\text{overlap}\,(g1, g2) \;=\; \frac{\sum\limits_{s \in g1 \cap g2} dom\,(s)}{\sum\limits_{s \in g1} dom\,(s)} \tag{43}$$

where *dom(s)* is the dominance of strand *s*. If overlap($g1,g2$) is greater than a threshold (currently set at 0.9), then $g1$ is removed from the set of groups. Note that this metric is not symmetric.

Subsumption is complicated by one further technicality. If two groups share a large number of elements, (i.e. overlap $(g1, g2) \approx$ overlap $(g2, g1) > 0.9$), then the selection of which group to remove is not arbitrary, since the pitch estimate from one group may be more reliable than that from the other. The solution is to retain pitch estimates from harmonic groups rather than those based on common AM.

One of the motivating factors for a subsumption principle, as discussed in chapter 4, was the likelihood that 'octave error groups' would be discovered due to the way in which a seed is interpreted as one of a number of possible harmonics or as the fundamental itself. Subsumption certainly removes some of these interpretations. The top right panel of Figure 5.8 shows the pitch contours which remain after subsumption is applied to those groups whose pitches are displayed in the top left panel. Several of the spurious groupings have been removed by subsumption. However, we cannot guarantee that all such octave errors will be removed, since higher estimates of the fundamental will lead to harmonic sieves whose slots reach to higher frequencies, hence possibly capturing components which would not form part of groups with lower fundamentals.

Pitch contour similarity

Groups remaining after subsumption are considered for fusion if their pitch contours are sufficiently close. The metric used has to be sufficiently wide to accommodate the lack of precision with which amplitude modulation rate is calculated. In the current system, a Gaussian-shaped scoring function like the one used to define AM rate similarity (39) is used to determine instant-by-instant similarity. The standard deviation of the Gaussian is 10 Hz. The total pitch contour

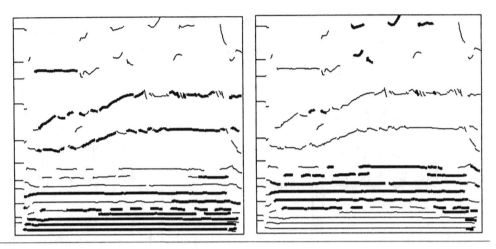

Figure 5.7 Combined groups for the /ru/-/li/ stimulus.

similarity between a pair of groups is the sum of these instantaneous similarities, divided by the number of frames in the overlap. The similarity score has to be above a threshold (0.7) for groups to be fused.

As explained in chapter 4, group combination takes place in an identical simultaneous/sequential constraint propagation framework to that used for first-level grouping. In practice, the most dominant group acts as a seed, and its pitch contour is compared with those of all overlapping groups.

The lower left panel of Figure 5.8 illustrates the pitch contours of combined groups. It is possible to see that some contours have been merged in the regions around 110 and 174 Hz (although some groups in those regions remain too erratic in pitch contour to be merged). Figure 5.7 shows the two main combined groups which result in the /ru/-/li/ example. Pitch contour similarity has been successful in merging harmonics in the F1 region with AM groups in the F3/F4 region.

The final stage of grouping is a second application of subsumption, this time using strands in combined groups. This is sometimes effective in removing groups. The lower right panel of Figure 5.8 shows the pitches remaining after the second stage of subsumption.

5.6 Grouping of natural speech signals

How effective is the model in determining which parts of a strand decomposition of speech belong together? Figure 5.9 shows strands before and after grouping in a voiced utterance. This figure is typical of the model's ability to find organisation in speech signals where no other source is present.

It is possible to listen to the results of grouping using resynthesis limited to those strands in the group. Speech signals resynthesised from groups are perfectly intelligible, appear to preserve speaker-specific cues, but sound slightly more muffled than the original. This can be partly accounted for by the tendency for high frequency strands to be rejected from groups, probably due to a difficulty in extracting reliable AM information in this region.

5.7 Discussion

The implementation of a structure for searching the auditory scene has been described in this chapter. As Figure 5.9 shows, it is possible to fuse most of the information in voiced speech into a single organisation using two basic grouping principles - harmonicity and common amplitude

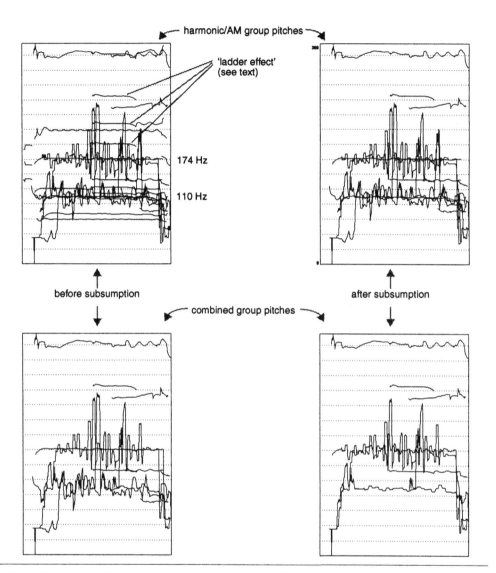

Figure 5.8   Derived pitches at various stages in grouping. *Top left*: pitch contours from harmonic and amplitude modulation groups. *Top right*: pitches after the first stage of subsumption. *Bottom left*: pitches of combined groups. *Bottom right*: pitches of combined groups after the second application of subsumption. Frequency axis divisions are 25 Hz apart.

modulation - together with a pitch contour similarity principle. This represents a lower-limit on performance of the system, and the introduction of such things as onset/offset synchrony will doubtless improve the system. What is of most interest is how well these principles work in recovering speech from a mixture. The system's ability to do this is examined in detail in the next chapter.

With the exception of the harmonic sieve implementation, the current system is forced to adopt arbitrary metrics and thresholds. Further experimental work will be required to replace these with principled mechanisms and values. The use of a wider 'mistuning' allowance for AM

Figure 5.9 Groups in natural speech signals. *Left*: strands prior to grouping. *Right*: the group which accounts for most of the evidence.

groups in comparison to that used in the harmonic sieve is based on Hoekstra and Ritsma [84] who showed that pitch estimates from unresolved components are less accurate than those based on resolved ones.

An inspection of Figure 5.8 suggests that it may be appropriate to smooth AM estimates prior to either grouping by common AM or integration by common pitch contour. No smoothing is present in the current model, and the evaluation presented in the next chapter might be improved if better estimates of AM could be obtained. Any smoothing would have to be quite severe to remove some of the erratic variation displayed in this figure.

Carlyon [22] has investigated the question of whether there are two separate pitch mechanisms, one temporal and based on unresolved components, the other spectral working on resolved harmonics. This question is currently of interest since autocorrelation approaches, described in chapter 1, propose that pitch can be extracted using a single mechanism. Carlyon performed a series of experiments in which listeners were asked to discriminate between pairs of complex sounds, each consisting of two groups of components. One group contained resolved partials of a harmonic series, whilst the other was filtered to contain representations in which harmonics were unresolved. His results led him to conclude that listeners can detect differences in F0 between such groups, and further, since all harmonics were frequency modulated coherently, such detection must have been based on simultaneous cross-spectral comparisons. Such results are compatible with autocorrelogram-based mechanisms, but could also be accounted for by the dual mechanism implemented here. An interesting quantitative result from Carlyon's study is that the threshold for detection of mistuning across frequency regions is around 6%. This is somewhat wider than the threshold for the detection of a mistuned harmonic, and suggests that any metric for integrating widely separated groups of components should be wider than that used to form harmonic groups. In the model described here, a standard deviation of 10 Hz in the Gaussian used to determine pitch similarity, combined with the threshold of 0.7, is roughly compatible with this.

Carlyon's study has a bearing on two other assumptions embodied in the work described here. The first involves the use of pitch trajectories as opposed to instantaneous pitch differences. Carlyon noted that listeners might be better at comparing the pitch trajectories of two groups of resolved components than they are at comparing the trajectories of one unresolved and one resolved group, and his experiment 5 tested for this possibility. However, the results suggested that listeners were not using this cue. So, although there are computational benefits from an early solution to auditory temporal correspondence, the auditory system may not be reliant on computing pitch contours. Further work is required to determine the stage at which temporal correspondences are made explicit in hearing.

The second factor concerns the way in which AM information is used. Carlyon noted that listeners might be able to use similarities in envelope repetition rate to bind together the output of low frequency channels (where beating is observable in the model) with that in higher frequency regions. His experiment 6 used stimuli in which the envelope repetition rate differed from the fundamental of the harmonic series. The results suggested that listeners were attending to F0 rather than to the rate of beating. In terms of the model described here, this would suggest that the search for groups with similar AM rate should be restricted to regions where components are not resolved. It also suggests that we should examine the use of envelope repetition rate as opposed to other cues for pitch determination of unresolved components.

The consideration of how AM is coded points out a limitation in the current model. There are three possible explanations for grouping by common AM. Two were described in section 5.3 - namely, common envelope repetition rate and common instant-by-instant amplitude fluctuations. A third is common periodicity - a cue which forms the basis for the autocorrelogram's ability to integrate information from unresolved channels. Whilst it would be possible to calculate the main periodicities in the model filters, then use them for grouping by AM, such an approach would be computationally expensive and, in any case, equivalent to the autocorrelogram mechanism.

One factor which differentiates the autocorrelation pitch estimation mechanism and the dual approach described here is the treatment of across frequency phase differences. The autocorrelogram is phase insensitive, at least for stimuli with periods greater than the autocorrelation width (which is usually about 20 ms, corresponding to an F0 of 50 Hz). Similarly, the envelope repetition metric (40) used here ignores phase differences. However, the similarity measure based on envelope fluctuation (42) is sensitive to differences in envelope phase. The study of Bregman et al. [15], described earlier, included one condition in which such phase differences appeared to result in weaker fusion of amplitude modulated tones. In that work, the AM rate was 100 Hz. However, later work has generated different conclusions. A further study by Carlyon [23] showed that whilst an envelope phase disparity for a fundamental of 20 Hz could be used by listeners to detect F0 difference, this was not the case at 125 Hz. However, a further experiment did show a beneficial effect of phase disparity up to a fundamental of 80 Hz. It is currently an open question as to whether these results can be explained by an autocorrelation mechanism.

A related point is the validity of, and necessity for, phase compensation used in the model. Listeners appear to be less reliant on phase differences in low frequency components than in higher frequency regions (Houtsma and Smurzynski [87]). It may not be appropriate to perform any phase correction at all in the model. This would have the effect of decoupling the low frequency region containing resolved components from the high frequency region, thereby restricting the search from common AM to high frequencies, as suggested by Carlyon's experiment 6. However, since significantly better correlations between, say, strands representing F3 and F4 are observed with phase correction, it is sensible to use phase alignment.

6

An evaluation of sound source separation in the model

6.1 Introduction

There are many possibilities for assessing computer models of auditory processes. Some of these are discussed in section 6.2. It is important to choose an evaluation technique whose results are directly interpretable with respect to the model. The method chosen in this study allows an answer to questions such as 'how much of an intrusive source is present in some grouping of components?' and 'what proportion of some source is explained by a particular group?'. The evaluation uses a set of speech signals mixed with a variety of other sources.

6.2 Evaluation methodologies

Five approaches to the evaluation of computer models of sound source separation are discussed below. The methods are compared with respect to such factors as interpretation and comparability of evaluation results, difficulty of application, stimulus restrictions and 'turnaround' time.

Comparing human and model performance on the same task

An example of this approach is the work of Assman and Summerfield [8], who compared the ability of listeners and four models of early auditory processing in the task of identifying each constituent of a synthetic double vowel pair. This work was reviewed in chapter 1. Perhaps the utility of this approach is its ability to apply a principle of falsifiability (Popper [138]) to models of auditory processing - a model may be abandoned or revised because its performance is radically different from that of listeners. This methodology is especially useful if first-order statistics - when performance is determined across a range of some stimulus variable such as difference in F0 - are available, as was the case in Assman and Summerfield's work.

The approach has some drawbacks. First, like any testing methodology, it cannot be used to confirm that a model is correct. Second, it is usually necessary to employ some kind of decision procedure to the model outputs in order to simulate cortical processing. This restricts the application of the approach to relatively simple tasks; experimental stimuli have to be carefully designed to prevent listeners using other cues provided by top-down processing.

Intelligibility testing

Separation performance can be assessed using intelligibility or recognition tests on signals before and after separation. This approach requires a resynthesis path from the separated representation. Stimulus design appears less critical in this task, since listeners exploit cues available in both the mixture and separated signal. Furthermore, it is possible to present results in terms of the improvement in signal-to-noise ratio, which is useful for comparison with other models. The approach may be time-consuming, and, like that outlined above, requires training in experimentation.

Recognition tests

An alternative to the employment of human subjects in intelligibility assessment is the use of machine recognisers. This is not restricted to speech stimuli, but could be applied to any type of source. This approach allows a choice of input representation to be supplied to the recogniser. It may be most straightforward to use resynthesised sources which can then be recognised by an unmodified recognition architecture (e.g. Weintraub [176]). Alternatively, recognition might use representations such as strands.

This approach can be applied automatically and is therefore likely to be tested on large data sets. Results can be expressed in terms of SNR improvement. However, interpretation of results may present problems. For example, there could be a mismatch between an auditory representation and the recognition architecture as has been recently illustrated by the ambiguous results obtained by several researchers who have compared recognition rates for speech processed by auditory and non-auditory front-ends (e.g. Hirahara and Iwamida [83]; Beet [10]). There is also a problem in relating the recognition *strategy* to that of humans.

Performance on specific tasks

The most extensive range of tests applied to a model of separation to date come from the work of Weintraub [176]. He evaluated the performance of his system on four specific tasks: tracking the pitch of two simultaneous talkers; determination of the number of speakers and their characteristics; spectral similarity of separated speech to original signal; and, digit recognition accuracy.

> Whilst the breadth of this approach is laudable, Weintraub himself makes the point that
>> The performance evaluation reflects how well these algorithms are able to achieve the different tasks, and does not directly reflect the ability of the theory to explain auditory sound separation. (p. 120)

It is just as well that this is the case, since otherwise the rather disappointing results obtained on some of his tasks would have unfortunate consequences for the health of the theory itself.

Mixture component identification

The assessment method adopted in this study attempts to avoid some of the problems inherent in techniques which provide indirect measures of the system's performance. The approach is to identify, in some representation of the mixture, those parts which arise due to one source and those which belong to other sources. In order to apply this technique, some automatic method of solving this *mixture correspondence problem* is required. The representations used in the model readily admit a solution to this problem, which is described in section 6.4.

The principle advantage of this approach is that it allows the derivation of easily interpreted metrics for performance assessment. The measures used here are described in section 6.5. For example, it is possible to state that a group contains some percentage of all mixture components belonging to one source. The approach is fully automated, allowing more extensive testing in any given time interval, and applies equally well to any type of acoustic source.

6.3 The mixture database

Other studies have concentrated on the separation of speech from other speech (e.g. Parsons [131]; Weintraub [176]). Yet, human performance is sufficiently flexible to allow robust perception of speech in a diverse acoustic environment. The model described in this thesis is primarily concerned with early auditory grouping, and, although speech specific factors may be present in the model, the intention is to model primitive grouping processes which should be neutral to the type of acoustic source. It is therefore appropriate to evaluate the model's performance on a wide range of possible source mixtures.

The model has been evaluated on a database of 100 mixtures, created by combining each of 10 natural, voiced utterances with each of 10 other signals, or *intrusions*. Two male speakers spoke the 5 sentences listed in Table 6.1. Fully voiced utterances were used because of the lack of any sequential integration in the model.

Table 6.1: Voiced sources

id	speaker	utterance
v0	1	I'll willingly marry Marilyn
v1	1	Why were you away a year, Roy?
v2	1	Why were you weary?
v3	1	Why were you all weary?
v4	1	Our lawyer will allow your rule
v5	2	I'll willingly marry Marilyn
v6	2	Why were you away a year, Roy?
v7	2	Why were you weary?
v8	2	Why were you all weary?
v9	2	Our lawyer will allow your rule

One characterisation of acoustic sources is the degree to which they are *narrow-* or *wide-* band, *continuous* or *interrupted*, *structured* or *unstructured*. The 10 intrusive sources selected

Table 6.2: Intrusive sources

id	description	characterisation
n0	1 kHz tone	narrowband, continuous, structured
n1	white noise	wideband, continuous, unstructured
n2	series of brief noise bursts	wideband, interrupted, unstructured
n3	teaching laboratory noise	wideband, continuous, partly structure
n4	new wave music	wideband, continuous, structured
n5	FM signal ("siren")	locally narrowband, continuous, structured
n6	telephone	wideband, interrupted, structured
n7	female TIMIT utterance	wideband, continuous, structured
n8	male TIMIT utterance	wideband, continuous, structured
n9	female utterance	wideband, continuous, structured

for this evaluation cover several different combinations of the above factors, as shown in Table 6.2; their waveforms (or portions of them) are shown in Figure 6.1. Synchrony strands representations of the intrusive sources presented alone are displayed in Figure 6.2.

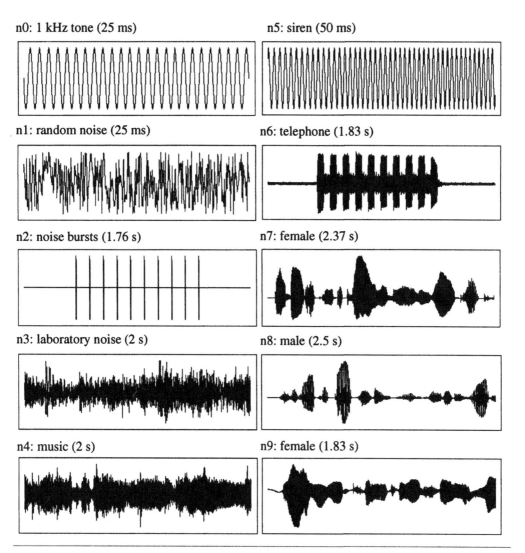

Figure 6.1   Waveforms representing fragments of the 10 intrusive sources.

An important factor in source separation is the relative level of each source in the mixture. Since the signals used here are non-stationary, the running short-term signal-to-noise ratio (SNR) is computed, using (44) below:

$$SNR(t) = 10\log 10\left(\frac{\sum_{i=0}^{w-1} s^2(t+i)}{\sum_{i=0}^{w-1} n^2(t+i)}\right) \tag{44}$$

where s and n represent the speech signal and intrusive sources respectively. Here, a 10 ms window is used. In cases where the intrusion had zero energy in a particular window, no SNR measurement was made (this occurs in intrusions n0, n2 and n5). Of particular interest are the

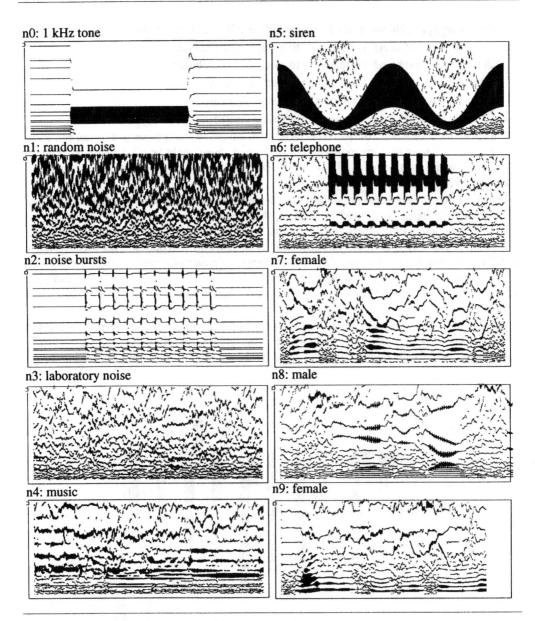

Figure 6.2 Synchrony strand representations of the 10 intrusive sources.

average and minimum values of *SNR(t)*. These are shown in Figure 6.3 for each noise condition - these figures represent an average over all voiced utterances.

6.4 The mixture correspondence problem

In order to assess the effectiveness of grouping in bringing together those parts of the auditory scene which belong to the same source, it is necessary to provide an automatic procedure which, given two sources A and B, identifies where each object in the mixture decomposition comes from. This correspondence problem is illustrated in Figure 6.4.

Consider the five possible ways in which elements in AB can correspond to elements of A[†]:

- A single element of AB corresponds to a single element of A.
- A single element of AB corresponds to more than one element of A.
- Several elements of AB correspond to a single element of A.
- Several elements of AB correspond to several elements of A.
- A single element of AB has no corresponding element in A.

If each element of AB is considered in turn, there are really just 3 cases to account for. First, that element may have no correspondence in A. Second, there might be a 1-1 mapping between that element and a member of A. Finally, there could be several objects in A which are candidates for correspondence.

On top of these, there is the possibility that elements in AB correspond to elements of A *and* B. This condition must be allowed for; in fact, the correspondence between AB and A is performed independently of that between AB and B. A further consideration is that correspondences will not, in general, be absolute - some flexibility in matching is required. This suggests that a solution to the correspondence problem should consist of a pair of mappings from elements of the mixture to a numerical indication of the degree to which that element belongs to A and/or B. For mix AB, these mappings can be represented by the functions ϕ_A, ϕ_B which map strands into the real interval [0,1].

The correspondence algorithm takes each strand in the mixture AB and computes the set of strands in A which are sufficiently similar to it. The criterion for similarity is detailed below. From this set, and for each time frame occupied by the strand, the *most similar* strand in the set

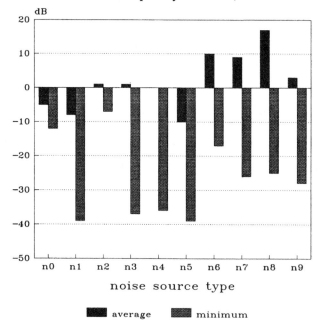

Figure 6.3 Average and minimum signal-to-noise ratios measured.

†. In the following description, A and B will denote the two sources, or representations thereof, whilst AB signifies the mixture of A and B.

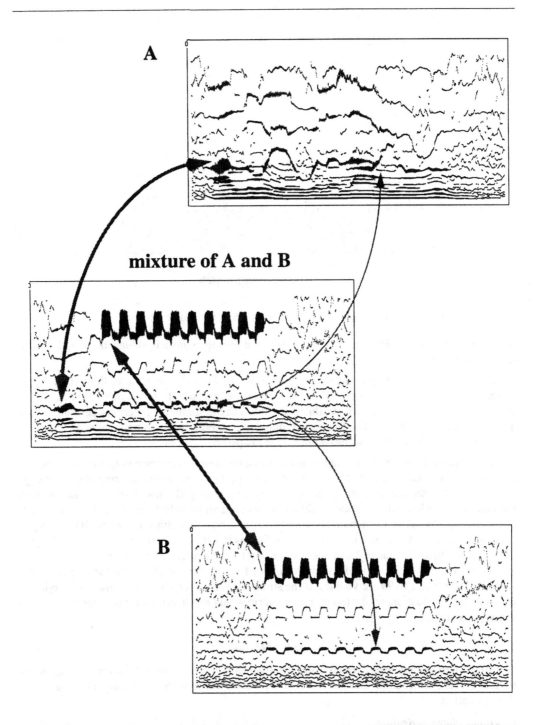

Figure 6.4 An illustration of the mixture correspondence problem. The central panel shows a mixture of speech plus telephone. Some components in this mixture can be readily associated with either of the two constituent sources, whilst others may belong to both in some proportion.

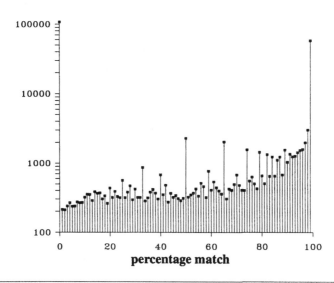

Figure 6.5 The distribution of matching scores over the whole of the mixture database.

is chosen to provide a similarity score. Finally, the average similarity along the length of the strand is calculated.

One metric suggested by auditory psychophysics is the width of slots in the hypothesised harmonic sieve used to determine whether a harmonic contributes to an estimate of pitch. In the absence of other compelling metrics, this was chosen as the similarity criterion operating across the whole frequency range. The metric is employed in precisely the same fashion as its use in the harmonicity grouping algorithm described in chapter 5.

As an indication of how well strands in a mix can be identified as coming from either constituent, Figure 6.5 shows a distribution of matching percentages obtained using the above approach. The distribution was compiled by simply aggregating the matching percentages from each strand in each mixture (a total of 226232 entries). If all strands were labelled as unambiguously coming from A or B, then this distribution would contain entries at 0% and 100% only. If strands represent constituents of A *and* B, then figures in between these extremes would be produced. The distribution clearly indicates that, using the similarity metric described above, most strands are thought to be derived solely from A or B (note the use of a log scale to ensure that values in the range 1 to 99 are visible). If the similarity metric were too wide, then we might expect a flatter distribution, whilst too narrow a metric would result in rather more bias towards the lower percentages.

6.5 Metrics

The strand correspondences derived using the algorithm described in the previous section allow several useful performance measures to be formulated. Three such metrics have been used for this evaluation.

Utterance characterisation

An ideal solution to the grouping problem in this evaluation consists of a group which characterises the *whole* of the voiced utterance (call it A), and contains no evidence for the intrusion B. The *characteristic* metric measures how many of the A's strands occurred in the group. This is not simply a counting process, but is weighted by a strand's dominance. Formally, the characteristic metric is defined as:

$$char\ (G)\ =\ \frac{\sum\limits_{s\in G}\phi_A(s)\,dom(s)}{\sum\limits_{s\in AB}\phi_A(s)\,dom(s)} \tag{45}$$

where G represents the group to be evaluated, and AB denotes the mix.

Positive evidence for the voiced source
The characteristic metric indicates how well a group represents all of the evidence for source A. However, it says nothing about the internal consistency of a group. This can be assessed by considering the positive evidence for A in a group, again weighted by dominance:

$$evid\ (G)\ =\ \frac{\sum\limits_{s\in G}\phi_A(s)\,dom(s)}{\sum\limits_{s\in G}dom(s)} \tag{46}$$

Crossover from the intrusive source
Perhaps the most important measure of grouping performance is the extent to which the intrusive source is excluded from a particular grouping. Some care is needed in providing an appropriate expression here. Some strands may belong to both A and B, and it would be a mistake to substitute B for A in (46) above since such strands would count as intrusions rather than as shared evidence. An alternative is to use the difference between ϕ_B and ϕ_A for each strand. If $\phi_A = 0$, this defaults to ϕ_B, whilst if $\phi_A = \phi_B = 0$, the shared intruder makes no contribution. The metric is:

$$crossover\ (G)\ =\ \frac{\sum\limits_{s\in G}max\,(0,\phi_B(s)-\phi_A(s))\,dom(s)}{\sum\limits_{s\in G}dom(s)} \tag{47}$$

6.6 Procedure

How are groups - G in the above metrics - selected from the output of the grouping algorithm, since this produces a *set* of groupings? Most such groups account for a small proportion of the evidence in the auditory scene. Furthermore, few span the whole time interval occupied by the signal. It is therefore possible to prune down the set of groups associated with each of the 100 mixtures by applying a simple criterion that the group must span at least 80% of the utterance. In general, this removes all but two or three groups for each mixture. In some cases, no group meets the spanning criterion. These mixtures (6% of the database, mainly involving intrusive source n3) were discounted in the evaluation since it is assumed that they represent not so much a failure in grouping but an incomplete set of grouping rules. For example, it might be possible to piece together several groups using rules for sequential integration.

A single group from the several spanning each mixture segregation is selected for the evaluation. In nearly all cases, the group which accounts for most of the evidence is chosen. In a small number of cases, all involving the artificial siren, the most dominant group corresponds to B. In all such cases, one of the other groups represented the voiced source A and was chosen for evaluation.

The three metrics produced similar results for each of the voiced utterances v0-v9 in most of the noise conditions n0-n9, so results are averaged across the v_i's.

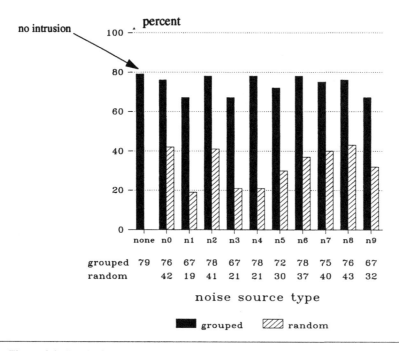

	none	n0	n1	n2	n3	n4	n5	n6	n7	n8	n9
grouped	79	76	67	78	67	78	72	78	75	76	67
random		42	19	41	21	21	30	37	40	43	32

noise source type

■ grouped   ▨ random

Figure 6.6 Results from the characterisation metric.

Before interpreting the results of applying the three metrics to such groups, it is necessary to consider two further measures which help in assessing the performance of the grouping algorithms.

Grouping at random

Suppose the system grouped objects randomly. How well would it perform under these conditions? In order to use this as a reference figure to show the advantage gained by grouping, for each group discovered, a group of the same size was chosen at random from the mixture. These random groups were then subjected to the same evaluation criteria as those produced *with* the application of grouping principles.

Grouping with no intrusions

If no intrusion is present (i.e. if B is null), then all the strands in the AB 'mix' should belong to A. However, the grouping principles implemented in the model may not be able to group all strands together. This may reflect factors such as representational deficiencies in strands, lack of coherence of modulation rate in the higher formants, or simply that strands will be formed even though no signal may be present (at the start and end of the utterance). Chapter 5 showed one such example of strands formed for a single utterance.

In order to provide an upper bound on expected characterisation performance, the best group found when no intrusion was present was evaluated using the characterisation metric (the other metrics are meaningless in this context, since none of B's strands are present). The results, averaged across the voiced utterances, are shown in the leftmost column of Figure 6.6.

6.7 Results

Utterance characterisation

When *no* intrusive source is present (leftmost bar in Figure 6.6), the model is able to form a group consisting of around four-fifths of the auditory scene. It may be surprising that this figure

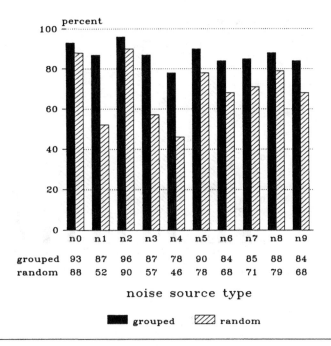

	n0	n1	n2	n3	n4	n5	n6	n7	n8	n9
grouped	93	87	96	87	78	90	84	85	88	84
random	88	52	90	57	46	78	68	71	79	68

noise source type

grouped   random

Figure 6.7 Results for the positive evidence metric.

is not somewhat higher, but examination of some such groups suggests that the higher frequency components are more difficult to recruit. This may be due to a poor representation of amplitude modulation in the higher formant regions of the model. Characterisation performance when no intrusion is present represents an informal upper bound on expected performance in the cases where other sources are present. In these cases, the model is able to group between 67% and 78% of the speech components, depending on the type of intrusive source. Performance is worst in the white noise and laboratory backgrounds, both of which had unfavourable signal-to-noise ratios, but encouragingly, near to the no-noise level for 6 out of 10 source types. In all conditions, performance is substantially better than would be expected if strands were allocated to groups at random, where characterisation rates vary from 19% to 43%.

Positive evidence for the voiced source

Grouped and random performance for the evidence metric are shown in Figure 6.7. This reflects the composition of groups and measures the percentage of elements which arise from the voiced source. Here, performance ranges from 84% to 96%. Again, results are better than random in all cases, although the high levels of performance in some random cases requires explanation. Consider noise source n0, the tonal component at 1 kHz. This is likely to be represented by a small number of strands, minimally a single strand. Hence, if a group is selected at random, it will tend to consist mainly of elements from the other source. The same argument applies to some of the other intrusions such as the siren.

Crossover from intrusive source

This is depicted in Figure 6.8. The degree to which the intrusive source appears in a group is largely the reverse of the positive evidence for that source. However, because of shared components, there is not a strict relationship between the two sets of figures. Least intrusion occurs for the sequence of tone bursts whilst grouping is least successful when the other source is music.

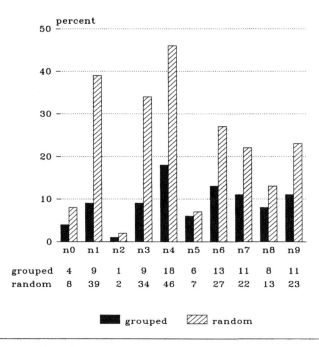

Figure 6.8 Crossover metric performance.

6.8 Illustrations of grouping

Figure 6.9 shows an example of the separation of speech from other speech. In this example, grouping has been quite successful in collecting together much of the information coming from the voiced source. Figure 6.10 shows an example where partial success is achieved. Here, the intrusion was laboratory noise, and the resulting mixture is depicted in the centre of the figure. Visually, the only organisation which is immediate is the harmonic set, which the algorithm has successfully extracted.

6.9 Discussion

This chapter has presented an evaluation of the model's ability to recover voiced speech from a variety of intrusive sources. The metrics chosen to illustrate the performance are easily interpretable. The model shows relatively uniform levels of performance across a range of intrusive conditions. In all conditions, the performance of the model is substantially better than random, so grouping is having a beneficial effect.

All 100 best groups have been resynthesised. Their quality ranges from totally intelligible through to almost incomprehensible (particularly the speech in white noise, although, for this mixture, the noise level is so high that the utterance is difficult to hear out of the raw mixture). In many cases, an impoverished strand representation (such as that shown in Figure 6.10) still produces an intelligible rendition, which indicates substantial amounts of top-down processing.

Intrusions which get through the grouping are clearly perceived as such, indicating that the principle of least commitment is not being applied sufficiently in the model.

One interesting effect arises in both the telephone and noise burst sequences. Often, the grouped result sounds as though a repetitive structure related to either type of intrusion remains. On examination of the strands associated with the group, the reason is apparent: segregating a rhythmic structure from a mixture often leaves a set of gaps with the same structure as the orig-

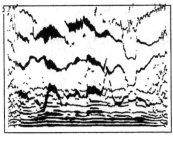
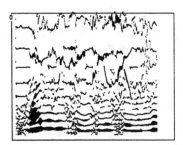
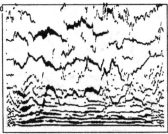
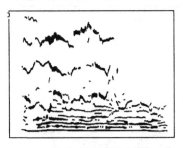

Figure 6.9 An illustration of grouping speech from a mixture. Here, the intrusion is itself speech. Strands for each utterance are shown at the top of the figure. The middle panel represents the strand analysis of the mixture. Organisation relating to both utterances is visible in the mixture, although the voiced utterance (as opposed to the intrusion) appears dominant. The lower panel represents the best grouping which is discovered in the mixture. Most of the strands in this group come from the voiced source.

inal. These are perceptually evident, and point to a need to perform some kind of extrapolation or sharing of energy. This latter point is a major limitation of the current model, and is due to the atomicity assumption expressed in chapter 4.

The results show the baseline performance of an untuned system, operating with a sparse collection of rules for organisation. They represent a useful reference against which future additions can be judged (see chapter 7 for a discussion of possible improvements and extensions to the model).

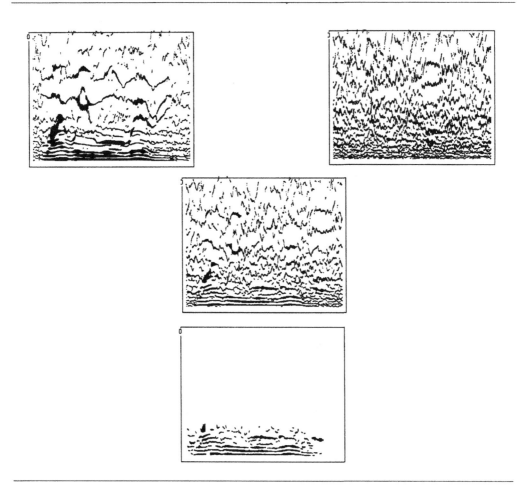

Figure 6.10 A further example of grouping. The intrusive source is laboratory noise. The best group contains harmonics from the speech source, although no information above the first formant region has been grouped.

7

Conclusions and further development

7.1 Summary of system

This thesis describes a computational system which seeks organisation in representations derived from a model of the auditory system. The initial processing step computes a decomposition of the signal into a collection of time-frequency descriptions called synchrony strands. This stage employs local similarity and continuity constraints to the outputs of a model of the auditory periphery, and aims to summarise the dominant periodic components as a function of time and frequency. The second processing step is to explore the decomposed representation, seeking coherent subsets of auditory objects. This is the stage at which auditory grouping principles are applied, and the current system is sufficiently flexible to accommodate several such rules for organisation within a common framework. The ability of the system to find organisation in complex acoustic signals has been evaluated. The main conclusion of this assessment was that the rules for grouping in the current implementation have a significant effect in accurately recombining decomposed evidence for the voiced speech source in a mixture.

7.2 Novelty of the approach

A distinctive feature of the model is its rich representational basis. The approach to auditory scene exploration used in this work would be infeasible without an early abstraction process operating upon the outputs of the periphery model. This abstraction process aims not only to preserve salient features, but also to make those very features explicit in the representation, whilst removing redundancy. This is accomplished in two stages. First, redundancy (similarity) in channel responses is summarised by exploiting an ordering constraint on the difference between channel centre frequency and the frequency to which the channel is responding. Then, first-order continuity constraints are applied to solve the auditory temporal correspondence problem. Properties such as frequency, amplitude and amplitude modulation rate are computed at each instant in time along the strand abstraction. Such properties are derived from all channels grouped together by similarity. In this way, strands represent a rich description of the signal, yet are sufficiently few in number to allow search strategies which attempt to explain each strand in the scene.

Synchrony strands arose as a result of grappling with the following problem: rules for auditory organisation are expressed in terms of frequency proximity, common AM rates, harmonicity, and so forth. But frequency or AM rate of *what*? Individual channels of auditory models, or some other abstraction? Channels are themselves an artifice, making no claim to model the numerosity of real auditory channels. Similarly, what justification can be found for a quantised, frame-based treatment of time? Just as most work in computer vision escapes from the artificial graticule of the bitmap relatively early in processing, the work described here moves quickly to an object-centred view of auditory processing. There is no claim that the auditory system computes strands or similar objects; strands are an abstraction, created to support a functional description of auditory grouping.

The principle advantage of the strand representation is the ease with which it allows auditory scene exploration to proceed. For example, it has been suggested that correlation of activity in widely separated frequency regions is of potential benefit in auditory segregation (Summerfield, Lea and Marshall [170]). Such cross-correlation of channels is prohibitively expensive, but strands can be correlated very rapidly. There seems to be little point in maintaining similar responses in neighbouring channels throughout the whole processing sequence.

As an example of the novel viewpoint afforded by a time-frequency representation, consider how the model might cope with the case of a vowel pair with crossing pitch contours. Figure 7.1 illustrates this case, and shows a solution which the auditory scene exploration process might find.

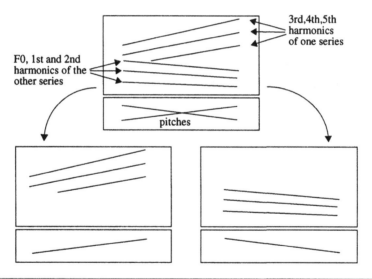

Figure 7.1 The separation of harmonic groups with crossing fundamentals.

Because the model summarises a single dominance in each frequency region, it will tend to represent the most dominant harmonics in any harmonic series. For vowels with reasonably separated first formants, this could give rise to the collection of resolved harmonics depicted schematically in the figure. The model would, in this case, have no problem in determining a pair of pitch contours, even though the fundamental frequencies cross. A system which performed separation on a frame-by-frame basis would have to solve a pitch correspondence problem in order to retrieve the two pitch contours.

This illustration leads to the prediction that double vowel separation is easier if the first formants are widely separated. Scheffers [150] presents results of listeners' vowel identification performance for each pair of vowels used in his study. Listeners' performance varies greatly across vowel pairs. If the results are plotted as a function of difference in F1, one might expect performance to increase as this difference gets greater. An informal analysis of his results supports this prediction.

7.3 Limitations of the model

Possible limitations of each processing stage were reviewed at the appropriate position in the text. Here, the main points are summarised.

The auditory filtering stage is based on linear filters. There is increasing evidence that the response of auditory nerve fibres is nonlinear, with broader tuning curves at high intensities.

The description-forming process which results in synchrony strands assumes that there is a single dominant resonance in each frequency channel, and that a summary of that dominance can be obtained from a contiguous section of the filterbank. This assumption is an approximation.

It is recognised that synchrony strands do not make explicit every kind of acoustic source component. For example, although whispered speech is adequately represented by strands for resynthesis, this is largely achieved through the use of a large number of objects; a simpler, more descriptive representation might be required. Similarly, onsets and offsets are not explicitly modelled.

Whilst groups can share objects in the current system, there is currently no mechanism for the allocation of energy to separate groups.

The model implements a small number of rules for organisation. In particular, no use is made of onset or offset synchrony.

The system is limited to primitive grouping, and makes no attempt to model schema-driven processes.

There is currently no model for competition. Similarly, no conflict resolution in, for example, harmonic labelling is implemented, although the constraint propagation framework described in chapter 4 would support such a scheme.

Finally, the model has to make some assumptions about similarity metrics which the auditory system might use to determine whether a pair of objects should be integrated.

Despite these current limitations, the model is sufficiently flexible to allow many of the above points to be addressed in future versions of the system. Some ideas for future work are discussed in 7.5.

7.4 Parsimony of explanation: The default condition of organisation

In the model, objects will remain segregated unless a reason can be found for fusing them with existing organisation. By contrast, it has been suggested that the default condition in auditory scene analysis is fusion (Bregman [17], p.334). Certainly, the auditory system appears to prefer a small number of explanations. The model does not claim to cover more than the first few stages of auditory organisation; later stages are needed to resolve competition, for example. However, to make fusion the default condition would have an effect on the algorithms used to perform grouping. One might imagine adopting a falsifiability criterion which segregates objects which are very unlikely to belong to a particular grouping (cf. Guzy and Edmonds [80]). At issue is whether it is easier to confidently group objects which have very similar properties over a time interval, or to remove components from a mixture because of dissimilarity. More experimental work is required to answer this question.

If the auditory system does prefer fusion, it might be possible to influence this by incorporating a metric on the length of explanations in the model. For example, the simplest label for a collection of randomly varying strands located within a closed time-frequency region might be 'fricated source'. Such an endeavour could be supported by the theoretical work of Wallace and

Georgeff [175] who define what constitutes an acceptable explanation of data, and use the length of explanation as a measure for selecting the best of a set of competing interpretations.

7.5 Further development of the model

Physiological models of auditory processing are increasingly sophisticated. Even during the period of the research described here, the focus of periphery models has changed from largely passive, filterbank systems to active cochlear simulations (e.g. Ambikairajah and Jones [5]; Neely [129]). Similarly, a greater number of attempts to model cells in the lower auditory brainstem nuclei, particularly at the cochlear nucleus level, are being reported (Ainsworth, Evans and Hackney [2]; Blackwood, Meyer and Ainsworth [11]; Meddis [123]). Any further development of the model should reflect what is known of auditory processing. One area where physiological investigations could usefully inform the model is in the extraction of onset and offset responses. Blackwood et al. describe a system for the processing of voiced plosives in which a single neuronal model is able to simulate most cochlear nucleus responses, including the onset response. Other work inspired by auditory topographic organisation, discussed in chapter 2, might provide a richer substrate on which to seek temporal correspondences. For example, maps of best amplitude modulation frequency as a function of spectral frequency could be used to support grouping by common AM.

At the other extreme of processing, there is considerable scope for extending the range of grouping principles in the model, although this activity relies to some extent on earlier description-making processes. One area which requires further work is sequential organisation. It is necessary to distinguish between the sequential grouping performed at a fine time scale in strand formation from the organisation of groups separated by larger intervals. There is a sizeable body of literature which addresses such processes in human perception. In particular, the effect of pitch contour continuity (e.g. Darwin and Bethell-Fox [34]) and spectral continuity (e.g. Cole and Scott [26]) have been studied.

In contrast to the work outlined above, which is concerned with primitive, bottom-up grouping, a more sophisticated model of perceptual organisation will need to cater for schema-driven grouping processes. It is clear that some (possibly a great deal) of the auditory system's ability to separate acoustic sources is due to prior, learned, representations or models of such sources. There is a limit to the grouping achievable using solely bottom-up processes. Possible modelling strategies range from generic learning architectures such as hidden Markov models and neural nets to causal or predictive models for acoustic sources.

The model could be extended to allow for the investigation of *auditory* as opposed to *acoustic*-phonetic coding. The prominence of the latter over the past 50 years was almost certainly due to the lack of computational models of auditory processing. It seems appropriate to study auditory-phonetic coding in the real world of speech mixed with other sources, processed by a separation model, rather than by examining 'clean' representations of 'clean' speech.

A

Filter derivations

This appendix contains derivations of results relating to the gammatone filter comparisons of Chapter 2. The starting point for the three approximation techniques is the low pass gammatone impulse response (which could be called the gamma response):

$$g_{lp}(t) = t^{n-1} e^{-bt} u(t) \tag{48}$$

Sections A.1 to A.3 give detailed derivations of the pole-mapping, bilinear transform and impulse invariance methods respectively. Section A.4 provides ideal responses, whilst section A.5 gives equations for calculating magnitude and phase responses of a digital filter.

A.1 Pole-mapping

In the pole-mapping technique, poles and zeros of the continuous domain transfer function are individually transformed into z-plane poles and zeros using the relationship

$$z = e^{sT} \tag{49}$$

where $s = j\omega$ and T is the sampling interval.

To see how this technique works in the case of the gammatone function, the impulse response of (48) must be transformed into an s-domain transfer function using the Laplace transform,

$$L(s) = \int_0^\infty f(t) e^{-j\omega t} dt \tag{50}$$

Using well-known properties of the Laplace transform, we have, for the gammatone envelope function $g_{lp}(t)$,

$$L(s) \propto \frac{1}{(s+b)^n} \tag{51}$$

Hence, the system has n poles at $s = -b$. Since b is real and positive, all poles lie on the negative real axis in the complex s-plane, and therefore map inside the unit circle in the z-plane, a property necessary for filter stability.

Using (49) above, each pole in the analogue filter maps to a pole at:

$$z = e^{-bT} \tag{52}$$

which leads to the following expression for the transfer function:

$$PM_n(z) \propto \left(\frac{z^{-1}}{1 - e^{-bT} z^{-1}} \right)^n \tag{53}$$

A.2 Bilinear transform

The bilinear transform method of digital approximation is a widely used technique which effectively compresses the whole of the imaginary axis in the s-plane into a single revolution of the unit circle in the z-plane, with everything in the left-half s-plane mapping inside the z-plane unit circle.

The bilinear transform is defined by the equations below:

$$s = \frac{2(1 - z^{-1})}{T(1 + z^{-1})} \tag{54}$$

$$z = \frac{1 + \dfrac{sT}{2}}{1 - \dfrac{sT}{2}} \tag{55}$$

where T is the reciprocal of the sampling frequency. For the gammatone function, whose Laplace transform is given above, the substitution of (54) leads to

$$BIL_n(z) = \frac{(n-1)!}{\left(\dfrac{2(1 - z^{-1})}{T(1 + z^{-1})} + b \right)^n} \tag{56}$$

which, with simple manipulation, gives

$$BIL_n(z) = (n-1)! \left(\frac{T(1 + z^{-1})}{\lambda + \mu z^{-1}} \right)^n \tag{57}$$

where

$$\lambda = bT + 2, \mu = bT - 2 \tag{58}$$

A more useful form for computational purposes is the equivalent expression:

$$BIL_n(z) \propto \frac{T^n \displaystyle\sum_{i=0}^{n} P_n(i+1) z^{-i}}{\lambda^n \displaystyle\sum_{i=0}^{n} \left(\frac{\mu}{\lambda} \right)^i P_n(i+1) z^{-i}} \tag{59}$$

where the $P_n(i)$ are coefficients of Pascal's triangle defined by

$$P_n(i) = P_{n-1}(i) + P_{n-1}(i-1) \text{ for } n > 1 \text{ and } 2 \leq i \leq n \tag{60}$$

$$P_n(1) = 1, \forall n$$

A.3 Impulse invariant transform

This method of digital approximation is derived from the observation that, in order to preserve the response of the analogue system to an impulse, the transfer function in the digital domain should be transformable into a sampled version of the actual impulse response. In other words, if $h_a(t)$ represents the response of the analogue filter to a unit impulse $\delta(t)$, then

$$H(z) = Z[h(m)] = Z[h_a(t)\big|_{t=mT}] \tag{61}$$

is the system function of the equivalent discrete-time filter. This suggests that we can characterise the impulse invariant transform of the gammatone filter as

$$IIT_n(z) = Z[g_{lp}(t)\big|_{t=mT}] \tag{62}$$

Hence, we need to find the Z-transform of

$$(mT)^{n-1}e^{-bmT}u(mT) \tag{63}$$

The following properties of the Z-transform (Ludeman [114]), together with its linearity, prove useful; $X(z)$ represents the Z-transform of $x(m)$:

$$Z[mx(m)] = -z\frac{d}{dz}X(z) \tag{64}$$

$$Z[a^m u(m)] = \frac{z}{z-a} \tag{65}$$

Rearranging equation (63) above leads to

$$T^{n-1}m^{n-1}u(mT)\left(e^{-bT}\right)^m \tag{66}$$

and applying the second property to the subexpression $u(mT)\left(e^{-bT}\right)^m$, we get

$$Z\left[\left(e^{-bT}\right)^m u(mT)\right] = \frac{z}{z-e^{-bT}} \tag{67}$$

This, combined with the linearity property, gives a transfer function for the first order filter

$$IIT_i(z) = \frac{z}{z-e^{-bT}} \tag{68}$$

or, in the more usual form, and substituting $a = e^{-bt}$,

$$IIT_1(z) = \frac{1}{1-az^{-1}} \tag{69}$$

Repeated application of property 1 leads to a succession of transfer functions for different values of n:

$$n = 2, \, IIT_2(z) = \frac{Taz^{-1}}{1-2az^{-1}+a^2z^{-2}} \tag{70}$$

$$n = 3, \, IIT_3(z) = \frac{T^2(az^{-1})(a+z^{-1})}{1-3az^{-1}+3a^2z^{-2}-a^3z^{-3}} \tag{71}$$

$$n = 4, \, IIT_4(z) = \frac{T^3(az^{-1})(a^2z^{-2}+4az^{-1}+1)}{1-4az^{-1}+6a^2z^{-2}-4a^3z^{-3}+a^4z^{-4}} \tag{72}$$

Transfer functions for higher-order filters are not difficult to obtain for specific values of n. Note that pole locations are identical to those produced by the pole-mapping approach.

A.4 Ideal responses

In this section, the ideal (analytic) expressions for the impulse, magnitude and phase responses are stated or derived.

Impulse response:

$$g_{lp}(t) = t^{n-1}e^{-bt}u(t) \tag{73}$$

Magnitude and phase responses:

From the Laplace transform given by equation (50), we remove imaginary parts from the denominator

$$H(j\omega) = \frac{(n-1)!}{(b+j\omega)^n} \frac{(b-j\omega)^n}{(b-j\omega)^n} \tag{74}$$

Hence

$$H(j\omega) = \frac{(n-1)!}{(b^2+\omega^2)^n}(b-j\omega)^n \tag{75}$$

The numerator can be rewritten as

$$(n-1)!b^n \sum_{i=0}^{n} P_n(i+1)(-\frac{j\omega}{b})^n \tag{76}$$

where $P_n(i)$ is the i-th element of the n-th row of Pascal's triangle. Real and imaginary parts are collected to give, for even n,

$$\Re = b^n \sum_{i=0}^{\frac{n}{2}} P_n(2i+1)(\frac{w}{b})^{2i}(-1)^i \tag{77}$$

$$\Im = b^n \sum_{i=0}^{\frac{n}{2}} P_n(2i)(\frac{w}{b})^{2i-1}(-1)^i \tag{78}$$

Trivial modifications will lead to the equivalent expressions for odd n. This leads to the following expressions for the ideal magnitude and phase responses:

$$|IDEAL_n(j\omega)| = \frac{(n-1)!\sqrt{\Re+\Im}}{(b^2+w^2)^n} \tag{79}$$

$$\phi_n = \operatorname{atan}\frac{\Im}{\Re} \tag{80}$$

A.5 Digital filter characteristics

In the case of the digital approximations, assuming for simplicity that the transfer function is in the general form below,

$$H(z) = \frac{\displaystyle\sum_{r=0}^{M} b_r z^{-r}}{\displaystyle\sum_{k=0}^{N} a_k z^{-k}} \tag{81}$$

the magnitude and phase responses are calculated using the standard formulae:

magnitude response of digital filter:

$$\left| H(e^{j\omega}) \right| = \left(\frac{\left(\displaystyle\sum_{r=0}^{M} b_r \cos r\omega\right)^2 + \left(\displaystyle\sum_{r=0}^{M} b_r \sin r\omega\right)^2}{\left(\displaystyle\sum_{k=0}^{N} a_k \cos k\omega\right)^2 + \left(\displaystyle\sum_{k=0}^{N} a_k \sin k\omega\right)^2} \right)^{1/2} \tag{82}$$

phase response of digital filter:

$$argHe^{j\omega} = atan\left(\frac{-\displaystyle\sum_{r=0}^{M} b_r \sin r\omega}{\displaystyle\sum_{r=0}^{M} b_r \cos r\omega} \right) - atan\left(\frac{-\displaystyle\sum_{k=0}^{N} a_k \sin k\omega}{\displaystyle\sum_{k=0}^{N} a_k \cos k\omega} \right) \tag{83}$$

Applying these to the cases of pole-mapping, bilinear transform and impulse invariance, it is possible to compare responses with the ideal.

B

Derivations relating to the hair cell model

B.1 Depletion and recovery for constant input

The equation for change in concentration in the immediate reservoir is:

$$\frac{dc_{imm}}{dt} = -kxc_{imm} + l(1 - c_{imm}) \tag{84}$$

which may be rearranged to give

$$\frac{dc_{imm}}{dt} + c_{imm}\lambda = l \tag{85}$$

Using the method of variation of parameter (Bajpai et al. [9]), the solution to this is of the form

$$c_{imm} = u(t) e^{-\lambda t} \tag{86}$$

where $u(t)$ can be found by differentiating the above expression and substituting in the original DE, viz:

$$e^{-\lambda t}(-\lambda u(t) + u'(t) - \lambda) = l \tag{87}$$

Hence $u'(t) = l e^{\lambda t}$, so

$$u(t) = \frac{l}{\lambda} e^{\lambda t} + c \tag{88}$$

leading to the solution

$$c_{imm} = \frac{l}{\lambda} + c e^{-\lambda t} \tag{89}$$

Initially, the concentration is unity, so c may be found to be $1 - \frac{l}{\lambda}$. Hence, the complete solution is

$$c_{imm} = \frac{l}{\lambda} + (1 - \frac{l}{\lambda}) e^{-\lambda t} \tag{90}$$

The solution to the recovery equation can be found similarly.

B.2 Time constants of adaptation and recovery

For adaptation, assume a concentration of unity at t=0. We therefore solve (90) for a concentration representing the mean of the initial and final concentrations:

$$\frac{1}{2}(1+\frac{l}{\lambda}) = \frac{l}{\lambda} + (1-\frac{l}{\lambda})e^{-\lambda\tau_{adapt}} \tag{91}$$

which, rearranging, leads to the adaptation time constant:

$$\tau_{adapt} = -\frac{1}{kx+l}\ln\frac{1}{2} \tag{92}$$

Similarly, for recovery, the initial concentration is given by the limit of

$$c_{imm} = 1 - \frac{kx}{kx+l}e^{-lt} \text{ as } t \to \infty \tag{93}$$

The final concentration is unity, hence

$$\frac{1}{2}(1+\frac{l}{\lambda}) = 1 - \frac{kx}{\lambda}e^{-l\tau_{recovery}} \tag{94}$$

leading to a recovery time constant

$$\tau_{recovery} = -\frac{1}{l}\ln\frac{1}{2} \tag{95}$$

C

Derivation of instantaneous frequency

The instantaneous frequency of the analytic signal is defined as the time derivative of instantaneous phase, which in turn is defined as:

$$\phi(t) = \operatorname{atan}\left[-\frac{H[s(t)]}{s(t)}\right] \tag{96}$$

The gammatone impulse response

$$g(t) = t^{n-1}e^{-bt}e^{i\omega t} \tag{97}$$

may be rewritten as

$$g(t) = a(t)\cos\omega t + ia(t)\sin\omega t \tag{98}$$

where $a(t) = t^{n-1}e^{-bt}$

To avoid having to compute the Hilbert transform explicitly, it is of interest to discover conditions for which the imaginary part of the gammatone filter is equal to (or closely approximates) the Hilbert transform of the real part of the filter. The insight here involves noting that the Hilbert transform shifts the phase of all components by + or -90 degrees, which is precisely the phase difference between the quadrature components sine and cosine. The first step is to examine the Hilbert transform of the real gammatone filter output. If $x(t)$ represents the input signal, the following property of the Hilbert transform means that the problem can be simplified to deal with an arbitrary input:

$$H[x(t) \bullet a(t)\cos\omega t] = x(t) \bullet H[a(t)\cos\omega t] \tag{99}$$

The definition of the Hilbert transform can now be used to produce

$$H[a(t)\cos\omega t] = -\frac{1}{\pi t} \bullet a(t)\cos\omega t \tag{100}$$

Using Fourier transforms to turn convolution into multiplication, this may be written as

$$F[H[a(t)\cos\omega t]] = F\left[-\frac{1}{\pi t}\right]F[a(t)\cos\omega t] \tag{101}$$

which is $i\operatorname{sgn}sF[a(t)\cos\omega t]$.

If we let $A(s)$ be the Fourier transform of a(t), then, by the modulation theorem

$$F[a(t)\cos\omega t] = \frac{1}{2}A(s - \frac{\omega}{2\pi}) + \frac{1}{2}A(s + \frac{\omega}{2\pi}) \qquad (102)$$

So, the RHS of (101) is

$$\frac{i\,\text{sgn}\,s}{2}(A(s - \frac{\omega}{2\pi}) + A(s + \frac{\omega}{2\pi})) \qquad (103)$$

Now consider the imaginary part of the gammatone: its Fourier transform is

$$\frac{-1}{2i}(A(s - \frac{\omega}{2\pi}) - A(s + \frac{\omega}{2\pi})) \qquad (104)$$

Multiplying top and bottom by i leads to

$$\frac{i}{2}(A(s + \frac{\omega}{2\pi}) - A(s - \frac{\omega}{2\pi})) \qquad (105)$$

It is now necessary to compare (103) with (105) to determine conditions under which they are equal, since these correspond to the imaginary part being equal to the Hilbert transform of the real part. If we insist that

$$A(s + \frac{\omega}{2\pi}) = 0 \text{ for } s \geq 0, \qquad (106)$$

and that

$$A(s - \frac{\omega}{2\pi}) = 0 \text{ when } s < 0, \qquad (107)$$

then the two equations are equal. This condition corresponds to a magnitude response which is bandlimited to the region

$$\left[-\frac{\omega}{2\pi}, \frac{\omega}{2\pi}\right]$$

where ω is the centre frequency of the filter. Does this apply to the filters used here? Examination of the magnitude response shown in Figure 2.2 suggests that the response will be greatly attenuated at filter CF, since we are using the *lowpass* gammatone. Hence, the gammatone filter is approximately bandlimited in the above region. Given that these conditions are met, instantaneous phase is

$$\phi(t) = \text{atan}\frac{-\Im(t)}{\Re(t)} \qquad (108)$$

and instantaneous frequency is its time derivative, which can be expressed in a computable form by differentiation, yielding

$$\sec^2\phi(t)\frac{d\phi}{dt} = \frac{d}{dt}(\frac{-\Im(t)}{\Re(t)}) \qquad (109)$$

This may be rewritten as

$$(1 + \tan^2\phi(t))\frac{d\phi}{dt} = \frac{1}{\Re^2(t)}(\Im(t)\frac{d}{dt}\Re(t) - \Re(t)\frac{d}{dt}\Im(t)) \qquad (110)$$

which, on substituting for $\tan\phi(t)$, becomes:

$$\left(1 + \frac{\Im^2(t)}{\Re^2(t)}\right)\frac{d\phi}{dt} = \frac{1}{\Re^2(t)}\left(\Im(t)\frac{d}{dt}\Re(t) - \Re(t)\frac{d}{dt}\Im(t)\right) \tag{111}$$

manipulation of which leads to:

$$\frac{d\phi}{dt} = \frac{1}{\Re^2(t) + \Im^2(t)}\left(\Im(t)\frac{d}{dt}\Re(t) - \Re(t)\frac{d}{dt}\Im(t)\right) \tag{112}$$

for $\Re(t) \neq 0$. Furthermore, since the gammatone filter is implemented by frequency shifting, the instantaneous frequency is determined by adding the centre frequency on to the above equation, leading to the expression given in the body of the thesis.

Bibliography

[1]   A.M.J.H. Aertsen and P.I.M. Johannesma (1980), 'Spectro-temporal receptive fields of auditory neurons in the grassfrog. I. Characterisation of tonal and natural stimuli', *Biol. Cybern.*, **38**, 223-234.

[2]   W.A. Ainsworth, E.F. Evans and C.M. Hackney[ed](in press), *Cochlear Nucleus: Structure and Function in Relation to Modelling*, JAI Press.

[3]   L.M. Aitkin (1986), *The Auditory Midbrain*, Clifton, NJ: Humana Press.

[4]   J.B. Allen (1985), 'Cochlear Modelling', *IEEE ASSP Magazine*, 3-29.

[5]   E. Ambikairajah and E. Jones (1990), 'An active cochlear model for speech recognition', *Proc. 3rd Australian Int. Conf. on Speech Science and Technology*, Melbourne, 130-135.

[6]   J. F. Ashmore (1987), 'A fast motile response in guinea-pig outer hair cells: The cellular basis of the cochlear amplifier', *J. Physiol.*, **388**, 323-347.

[7]   P.F. Assman and Q. Summerfield (1989), 'Modelling the perception of concurrent vowels: Vowels with the same fundamental frequency', *J. Acoust. Soc. Am.*, **85**, 327-338.

[8]   P.F. Assman and Q. Summerfield (1990), 'Modelling the perception of concurrent vowels: Vowels with different fundamental frequencies', *J. Acoust. Soc. Am.*, **88**, 680-697.

[9]   A.C. Bajpai, I.M. Calus, J.A. Fairley and D. Walker (1973), *Mathematics for Engineers and Scientists*, Volume 2, John Wiley.

[10] S.W. Beet (1990), 'Automatic speech recognition using a reduced auditory representation and position-tolerant discrimination', *Computer Speech & Language*, **4**, 1, 17-33.

[11] N Blackwood, G. Meyer and W.A. Ainsworth (1990), 'A model of the processing of voiced plosives in the auditory nerve and cochlear nucleus', *Proc. Inst. of Acoustics*, **12**,10, 423-430.

[12] M. Blomberg, R. Carlson, K. Elenius and B. Granstrom (1986), 'Auditory models as front ends in speech recognition systems', in: *Invariance and Variability in Speech Processes*, J.S. Perkell et al. (eds), Lawrence Erlbaum Associates.

[13] R. Bracewell (1986), *The Fourier Transform and its Applications*, McGraw-Hill.

[14] A.S. Bregman and S. Pinker (1978), 'Auditory streaming and the building of timbre', *Can. Jnl. Psych.*, **32**, 19-31.

[15] A.S. Bregman, J. Abramson, P. Doehring and C.J. Darwin (1985), 'Spectral integration based on common amplitude modulation', *Perception and Psychophysics*, **37**, 483-493.

[16] A.S. Bregman, R. Levitan and C. Liao (1990), 'Fusion of auditory components: Effect of the frequency of amplitude modulation', *Perception and Psychophysics*, **47**, 68-73.

[17] A.S. Bregman (1990), *Auditory Scene Analysis*, MIT Press.

[18] R. Britt and A. Starr (1975), 'Synaptic events and discharge patterns of cochlear nucleus cells. I. Steady-frequency tone bursts', *J. Neurophys.*, **39**, 162-178.

[19] R. Britt and A. Starr (1975), 'Synaptic events and discharge patterns of cochlear nucleus cells. II. Frequency-modulated tones', *J. Neurophys.*, **39**, 179-194.

[20] W.E. Brownell, C.R. Bader, D. Bertrand and Y. Ribaupierre (1985), 'Evoked mechanical responses of isolated cochlear outer hair cells', *Science*, **277**, 194-196.

[21] R. Carlson and B. Granstrom (1982), 'Towards an auditory spectrograph', in: *The Representation of Speech in the Peripheral Auditory System*, R. Carlson and B. Granstrom (eds), Elsevier.

[22] R.P. Carlyon, L. Demars and C. Semal (1992), 'Detection of across-frequency differences in fundamental frequency', *J. Acoust. Soc. Am.*, **91(1)**, 279-292.

[23] R.P. Carlyon (1991), 'Detection of F0 differences and envelope asynchronies between pairs of simultaneous formant-like sounds', *Poster presented at a meeting of the Institute of Acoustics Speech Group on Perceptual Separation of Sound Sources*, University of Sussex, Feb.

[24] L.A. Chistovitch (1974), 'A functional model of signal processing in the peripheral auditory system', *Acustica*, **31**, 6, 349-354.

[25] V. Ciocca and A.S. Bregman (1987), 'Perceived continuity of gliding and steady-state tones through interrupting noise', *Perception and Psychophysics*, **42**, 476-484.

[26] R.A. Cole and B. Scott (1973), 'Perception of temporal order in speech', *Can. J. Psych.*, **27**, 441-449.

[27] M.P. Cooke (1986), 'A computer model of peripheral auditory processing incorporating phase-locking, suppression and adaptation effects', *Speech Communication*, **5**, 261-281.

[28] M.P. Cooke and P.D. Green (1987), 'On finding objects in spectrograms: A multiscale, relaxation labelling approach', in: *Recent Advances in Speech Understanding and Dialog Systems*, H. Niemann, M. Lang and G. Sagerer (eds), Springer-Verlag.

[29] M.P. Cooke (1988), 'Exploiting early constraints in speech analysis', *Proc. 7th FASE Symposium*, Edinburgh, 803-809.

[30] M.P. Cooke and P.D. Green (1990), 'The auditory speech sketch', *Proc. Institute of Acoustics*, **12**, 10, 355-362.

[31] A.D. Crawford and R. Fettiplace (1981), 'Nonlinearities in the response of turtle hair cells', *J. Physiol.*, **315**, 317-338.

[32] P. Dallos (1970), 'Low frequency auditory characteristics: species dependence', *J. Acoust. Soc. Am.*, **48**, 489-499.

[33] R.I. Damper, R.A.W. Bladon, R.W. Hukin and G.N.A. Irvine (1987), 'Resynthesis and matching experiments on an auditory theory of male/female normalisation', *Proc. 11th Int. Congress Phonetic Sciences*, Tallinn, paper SE 60.4.

[34] C.J. Darwin and C.E. Bethell-Fox (1977), 'Pitch continuity and speech source attribution', *J. Exp. Psy.: Human Perception and Performance*, **3**, 665-672.

[35] C.J. Darwin (1981),'Perceptual grouping of speech components differing in fundamental frequency and onset time', *Quart. Jnl. Exp. Psych.*, **33A**, 185-207.

[36] C.J. Darwin (1982), 'Hearing voices: auditory and phonetic constraints in speech perception', unpublished manuscript.

[37] C.J. Darwin (1983), 'Auditory processing and speech perception', in: *Attention and performance X*, D.G. Bouwhuis (ed), Erlbaum, Hillsdale, NJ.

[38] C.J. Darwin (1984), 'Perceiving vowels in the presence of another sound: constraints on formant perception', *J. Acoust. Soc. Am.*, **76**(6), 1636-1647.

[39] C.J. Darwin and N.S. Sutherland (1984), 'Grouping frequency components of vowels: when is a harmonic not a harmonic ?', *Quart. Jnl. Exp. Psych.*, **36A**, 193-208.

[40] C.J. Darwin and R.B. Gardner (1986), 'Mistuning a harmonic of a vowel: grouping and phase effects on vowel quality', *J. Acoust. Soc. Am.*, **79**, 838-845.

[41] C.J. Darwin and J. Stone (1986), Personal communication.

[42] C.J. Darwin and R.B. Gardner (1987), 'Perceptual separation of speech from concurrent sounds', *The Psychophysics of Speech Perception*, M.E.H. Schouten (ed), Martinus Nijhoff, 112-124.

[43] C.J. Darwin, H.Pattison and R.B. Gardner (1989), 'Vowel quality changes produced by surrounding tone sequences', *Perception and Psychophysics*, **45**, 333-342.

[44] E. de Boer and P. Kuyper (1968), 'Triggered correlation', *IEEE Trans. Biomed. Eng.*, BME-**15**, 169-179.

[45] E. de Boer and H.R. de Jongh (1978), 'On cochlear encoding: potentialities and limitations of the reverse-correlation technique', *J. Acoust. Soc. Am.*, **63**, 115-135.

[46] E. de Boer (1983), 'On active and passive cochlear models - towards a generalised analysis', *J. Acoust. Soc. Am.*, **73**, 574-576.

[47] E. de Boer and C. Kruidenier (1990), 'On the ringing limits of the auditory periphery', *Biol. Cybern.* , **63**, 433-442.

[48] L. de No (1981), *The Primary Acoustic Nuclei*, Raven Press.

[49] B. Delgutte (1982), 'Some correlates of phonetic distinctions at the level of the auditory nerve', in: *The Representation of Speech in the Peripheral Auditory System*, R. Carlson and B. Granstrom (eds), Elsevier, Amsterdam.

[50] L. Deng, C.D. Geisler and S. Greenberg (1988), 'A composite model of the auditory periphery for the processing of speech', *J. Phonetics*, **16**, 93-108.

[51] J.M. Dolmazon, L. Bastet and V.S. Shupljakov (1977), 'A functional model of the peripheral auditory system in speech processing', *Proc. IEEE Int. Conf. Acoustics, Speech and Signal Processing*, Hartford, 261-264.

[52] R.O. Duda and P.E. Hart (1973), *Pattern Recognition and Scene Analysis*, New York: Wiley.

[53] R.O. Duda, R.F. Lyon and M. Slaney (1990), 'Correlograms and the separation of sounds', *Proc. Asilomar Annual Conf. on Signals, Systems and Computers*.

[54] H. Duifhuis, L.F. Willems and R.J. Sluyter (1982), 'Measurement of pitch in speech: an implementation of Goldstein's theory of pitch perception', *J. Acoust. Soc. Am.*, **71**, 1568-1580.

[55] H. Duifhuis and A.W. Bezemer (1983), 'Peripheral auditory adaptation and forward masking', in: *Hearing - Physiological Bases and Psychophysics*, R. Klinke and R. Hartmann (eds), Springer, Berlin.

[56] L.D. Erman, F. Hayes-Roth, V. Lesser and R. Reddy (1980), 'The HEARSAY-II speech understanding system: Integrating knowledge to resolve uncertainty', *ACM Computing Surveys*, **12**, 213-253.

[57] E.F. Evans (1980), 'An electronic analogue of single unit recording from the cochlear nerve for teaching and research', *J. Physiol.*, **298**, 6-7.

[58] E. Evans (1986), 'Cochlear nerve fibre temporal discharge patterns, cochlear frequency selectivity and the dominant region for pitch', in: *Auditory Frequency Selectivity*, B.C.J. Moore and R.D. Patterson (eds), Plenum Publishing Corporation.

[59] G. Fant (1989), 'Speech research in perspective', *Proc. European Conference on Speech Communication and Technology*, Paris, 3-4.

[60] F.K. Fink and P. Dalsgaard (1989), 'Estimation of formants in noise corrupted speech using auditory models', *Proc. European Conference on Speech Communication and Technology*, Paris, 677-680.

[61] A. Flock and D. Strelioff (1984), 'Graded and nonlinear mechanical properties of sensory hairs in the mammalian hearing organ', *Nature*, **310**(16), 597-599.

[62] D. H. Friedman (1985), 'Instantaneous-frequency distribution vs. time: An interpretation of the phase structure of speech', *Proc. IEEE Int. Conf. Acoustics, Speech and Signal Processing*, paper 29.10.

[63] T. Furukawa, Y. Hayashida and S. Matsuura (1978), 'Quantal analysis of the size of excitatory post-synaptic potentials at synapses between hair cells and afferent nerve fibres in goldfish', *J. Physiol.*, **276**, 211-226.

[64] R.B. Gardner and C.J. Darwin (1986), 'Grouping of vowel harmonics by frequency modulation: absence of effects on phonemic categorisation', *Perception and Psychophysics*, **40**, 183-187.

[65] R.B. Gardner, S. A. Gaskill and C.J. Darwin (1989),'Perceptual grouping of formants with static and dynamic differences in fundamental frequency', *J. Acoust. Soc. Am.*, **85**, 3, 1329-1337.

[66] M.R. Garey and D.S. Johnson (1979), *Computers and Intractability: A Guide to NP-Completeness*, W.H. Freeman, San Francisco.

[67] J.S. Garofolo and D.S. Pallett (1989), 'Use of CD-ROM for speech database storage and exchange', *Proc. European Conference on Speech Communication and Technology*, Paris, 309-315.

[68] C.D. Geisler (1988), 'Representation of speech sounds in the auditory periphery', *J. Phonetics*, **16**, 19-35.

[69] O. Ghitza (1986), 'Speech analysis/synthesis based on matching the synthesised and original representation in the auditory-nerve level', *Proc. IEEE Int. Conf. Acoustics, Speech and Signal Processing*, paper 37.11.

[70] O. Ghitza (1988), 'Temporal non-place information in the auditory nerve firing patterns as a front end for speech recognition in a noisy environment', *J. Phonetics*, **16**, 109-123.

[71] J.J. Gibson (1979), *The Ecological Approach to Visual Perception*, Houghton-Mifflin.

[72] D.A. Godfrey, N.Y.S. Kiang and B.E. Norris (1975), 'Single unit activity in the posteroventral cochlear nucleus of the cat', *J. Comp. Neur.*, **162**, 247-268.

[73] R. Goldhor (1983), 'A speech signal processing system based on a peripheral auditory model', *Proc. IEEE Int. Conf. Acoustics, Speech and Signal Processing*, Boston, 1368-1371.

[74] M.J. Goldsmith (1989), 'Speech databases for UK speech technology and research: A survey of resources and future needs', *UK National Physical Laboratory Report RSA(EXT)010*, HMSO.

[75] J.L. Goldstein (1973), 'An optimum processor theory for the central formation of the pitch of complex tones', *J. Acoust. Soc. Am.*, **54**, 1496-1516.

[76] P.D. Green and P.J. Grace (1981), 'A descriptive apporach to computer speech understanding', *Proc. Inst. Acoustics*, 261-264.

[77] P.D. Green and A.R. Wood (1984), 'Knowledge-based speech understanding: Towards a representational approach', *Proc. 6th European Conf. on Artificial Intelligence*, Pisa, 337-340.

[78] P.D. Green and A.R. Wood (1986), 'A representational approach to knowledge-based acoustic-phonetic processing in speech recognition', *Proc. IEEE Int. Conf. Acoustics, Speech and Signal Processing*, Tokyo, paper 23.4.

[79] P.D. Green, G.J. Brown, M.P. Cooke, M.D. Crawford and A.J.H. Simons (1990), 'Bridging the gap between signals and symbols in speech recognition', in: *Advances in Speech, Hearing and Language Processing*, W.A. Ainsworth (ed), JAI Press.

[80] J.J. Guzy and E.A. Edmonds (1986), 'Definitely not pattern matching: a method in automatic speech recognition', *Proc. Inst. Acoustics*, **8**, 7, 425-442.

[81] C.M. Hackney (1987), 'Anatomical features of the auditory pathway from cochlea to cortex', *Brit. Med. Bull.*, **43**, 4, 780-801.

[82] M.J. Hewitt and R. Meddis (1991), 'An evaluation of eight computer models of mammalian inner hair-cell function', *J. Acoust. Soc. Am.*, **90**(2), 904-917.

[83] T. Hirahara and H. Iwamida (1990), 'Auditory spectrograms in HMM phoneme recognition', *Proc. Int. Conf. on Spoken Language Processing*, Kobe, 381-384.

[84] A. Hoekstra and R.J. Ritsma (1977), 'Perceptive hearing loss and frequency selectivity', in: *The Psychophysics and Physiology of Hearing*, E.F. Evans and J.P. Wilson (eds), Academic Press.

[85] J. Holdsworth, I. Nimmo-Smith, R. Patterson and P. Rice (1988), 'Implementing a GammaTone filter bank', Personal communication.

[86] M.H. Holmes and J.D. Cole (1984), 'Cochlear mechanics: analysis for a pure tone', *J. Acoust. Soc. Am.*, **76**, 767-778.

[87] A.J.M. Houtsma and J. Smurzynski (1990), 'Pitch identification and discrimination for complex tones with many harmonics', *J. Acoust. Soc. Am.*, **87**, 304-310.

[88] A.J. Hudspeth and D.P. Corey (1977), 'Sensitivity, polarity and conductance change in the response of vertebrate hair cells to controlled mechanical stimuli', *Proc. Nat. Ac. Sci.*, USA, **74**, 2407-2411.

[89] R. Hukin and R.I. Damper (1989), 'Testing an auditory model by resynthesis', *Proc. European Conference on Speech Communication and Technology*, Paris, 243-246.

[90] M. J. Hunt and C. Lefebvre (1986), 'Speech recognition using a cochlear model', *Proc. IEEE Int. Conf. Acoustics, Speech and Signal Processing*, 1979-1982.

[91] D.R.F. Irvine (1986), *The Auditory Brainstem*, Berlin: Springer Verlag.

[92] D.H. Johnson (1980), 'The relationship between spike rate and synchrony in responses of auditory-nerve fibres to single tones', *J. Acoust. Soc. Am.*, **68**, 1115-1122.

[93]   D.H. Johnson and A. Swami (1983), 'The transmission of signals by auditory-nerve fibre discharge patterns', *J. Acoust. Soc. Am.*, **74**, 493-501.

[94]   B.M. Johnstone, R. Patuzzi and G.K. Yates (1986), 'Basilar membrane measurements and the travelling wave', *Hearing Research*, **22**, 147-153.

[95]   M. Karjalaienen (1984), 'Sound quality measurements of audio systems based on models of auditory perception', *Proc. IEEE Int. Conf. Acoustics, Speech and Signal Processing*, paper 19.9.

[96]   M. Karjalainen (1987), 'Auditory models for speech processing', *Proc. 11th Int. Congress Phonetic Sciences*, Tallinn, paper SE 82.1.

[97]   R.M. Karp (1977), 'The probabilistic analysis of partitioning algorithms for the travelling salesman problem in the plane', *Math. Oper. Res.*, **2**, 209-224.

[98]   D.T. Kemp (1978), 'Stimulated acoustic emissions from within the human auditory system', *J. Acoust. Soc. Am.*, **64**, 1386-1391.

[99]   N.Y.S. Kiang, T. Watanabe, E.C. Thomas and L.F. Clark (1965), *Discharge Patterns of Single Fibres in the Cat's Auditory Nerve*, MIT Press, Cambridge, MA.

[100] N.Y.S. Kiang and E.C. Moxon (1974), 'Tails of tuning curves of auditory-nerve fibres', *J. Acoust. Soc. Am.*, **55**, 620-630.

[101] D. Klatt (1980), 'Software for a cascade/parallel formant synthesiser'', *J. Acoust. Soc. Am*, **67**, 3, 971-995.

[102] Y. Laprie, J-P. Haton and J-M. Pierrel (1990), 'Phonetic triplets in knowledge based approach of acoustic-phonetic decoding', *Proc. Int. Conf. on Spoken Language Processing*, Kobe, 365-368.

[103] E.L. Lawler (1985), *The Travelling Salesman Problem: A Guided Tour of Combinatorial Optimisation*, John Wiley, New York.

[104] D.G.B. Leonard and S.M. Khanna (1984), 'Histological evaluation of damage in cat cochleas used for measurement of basilar membrane mechanics', *J. Acoust. Soc. Am.*, **75**, 523-527.

[105] H.C. Leung and V.W. Zue (1986), 'Visual characterisation of speech spectrograms', *Proc. IEEE Int. Conf. Acoustics, Speech and Signal Processing*, paper 51.1.

[106] M.C. Liberman (1978), 'Auditory-nerve responses from cats raised in a low-noise chamber', *J. Acoust. Soc. Am.*, **63**, 442-455.

[107] M.C. Liberman (1982), 'The cochlear frequency map for the cat: Labelling auditory nerve fibres of known characteristic frequency', *J. Acoust. Soc. Am.*, **72**, 1441-1449.

[108] A.M. Liberman (1982), 'On finding that speech is special', *Am. Psych.*, **37**, 148-167.

[109] J-S. Lienard (1987), 'Speech analysis and reconstruction using short-time, elementary waveforms', *Proc. IEEE Int. Conf. Acoustics, Speech and Signal Processing*, 948-951.

[110] R.F. Lyon (1982), 'A computational model of filtering, detection and compression in the cochlea', *Proc. IEEE Int. Conf. Acoustics, Speech and Signal Processing*, Paris, 1282-1285.

[111] R.F. Lyon (1983), 'A computational model of binaural localisation and separation', *Proc. IEEE Int. Conf. Acoustics, Speech and Signal Processing*, Boston, 1148-1151.

[112] R.F. Lyon (1984), 'Computational models of neural auditory processing, *Proc. IEEE Int. Conf. Acoustics, Speech and Signal Processing*, San Diego.

[113] R.F. Lyon and L. Dyer (1986), 'Experiments with a computational model of the cochlea', *Proc. IEEE Int. Conf. Acoustics, Speech and Signal Processing*, Toyko, 1975-1978.

[114] L. C. Ludeman (1987), *Fundamentals of Digital Signal Processing*, John Wiley.

[115] S. McAdams (1984), *Spectral Fusion, Spectral Parsing and the Formation of Auditory Images*, Ph. D. Thesis, Stanford University.

[116] S. McAdams (1989), 'Segregation of concurrent sounds. I: Effects of frequency modulation coherence', *J. Acoust. Soc. Am.*, **86**, 2148-2159.

[117] D. Marr (1976), 'Early processing of visual information', *Philosophical Transactions of the Royal Society*, B, **275**, 483-519.

[118] D. Marr (1982), *Vision*, W.H. Freeman.

[119] R. Meddis (1986), 'Simulation of mechanical to neural transduction in the auditory receptor', *J. Acoust. Soc. Am.*, **79**, 702-711.

[120] R. Meddis (1986), 'Comments on "Very rapid adaptation in the guinea pig auditory nerve"', *Hearing Research*, **23**, 287-288.

[121] R. Meddis (1988), 'Simulation of auditory-neural transduction: Further studies', *J. Acoust. Soc. Am.*, **83**, 1056-1063.

[122] R. Meddis and M. J. Hewitt (1992), 'Modelling the identification of concurrent vowels with different fundamental frequencies', *J. Acoust. Soc. Am.*, **91**(1), 233-245.

[123] R.Meddis (in press), 'A physiological model of auditory selective attention', in: *Cochlear Nucleus: Structure and Function in Relation to Modelling*, W.A. Ainsworth, E.F. Evans and C.M. Hackney (eds), JAI Press.

[124] A. Moller (1970), 'Two different types of frequency selective neurons in the cochlear nucleus of the rat', in: *Frequency Analysis and Periodicity Detection in Hearing*, R. Plomp and G.F. Smoorenburg (eds), Leiden: Sijthoff.

[125] B.C.J. Moore and B.R. Glasberg (1983), 'Suggested formulae for calculating auditory-filter bandwidths and excitation patterns', *J. Acoust. Soc. Am.*, **74**, 3, 750-753.

[126] B.C.J. Moore, R.W. Peters and B.R. Glasberg (1985), 'Relative dominance of individual partials in determining the pitch of complex tones', *J. Acoust. Soc. Am.*, **77**, 1853-1860.

[127] D.R. Moore (1987), 'Physiology of higher auditory system', *Brit. Med. Bull.*, **43**, 4, 856-870.

[128] R.K. Moore, A.P. Varga and M. Kadirkamanatha (1991), 'Automatic separation of speech and other complex sounds using hidden Markov model decomposition', *paper presented at meeting of the Institute of Acoustics Speech Group*, Sussex University, Feb. 27.

[129] S.T. Neely (1989), 'A model for bidirectional transduction in outer hair cells', in: *Cochlear Mechanisms*, J.P. Wilson and D.T. Kemp (eds), Plenum, 75-82.

[130] Y. Oonu and Y. Sujaku (1975), 'A model for automatic gain control observed in the firings of primary auditory neurons', *Trans. IECE(Japan)*, **58**, 352-358.

[131] T.W. Parsons (1976), 'Separation of speech from interfering sounds by means of harmonic selection', *J. Acoust. Soc. Am.*, **60**, 911-918.

[132] R.D. Patterson (1976), 'Auditory filter shapes derived with noise stimuli', *J. Acoust. Soc. Am.*, **59**, 640-654.

[133] R. Patterson, I. Nimmo-Smith, J. Holdsworth and P. Rice (1987), 'An efficient auditory filterbank based on the GammaTone function', *paper presented at a meeting of the Institute of Acoustics Speech Group on Auditory Modelling*, RSRE, Dec. 14-15.

[134] J.O. Pickles (1988), *An Introduction to the Physiology of Hearing*, 2nd Edition, Academic Press.

[135] T. Poggio, V. Torre and C. Koch (1985), 'Computational vision and regularisation theory', *Nature*, **317**, 26, 314-319.

[136] M.J. Pont and R.I. Damper (1988), 'A neural model of infant speech perception', *Proc. 7th FASE symposium, Edinburgh*, 515-522.

[137] M.J. Pont (1989), *The Role of the Dorsal Cochlear Nucleus in the Perception of Voicing Contrasts in Initial English Stop Consonants: A Computational Modelling Study*, Ph.D. Thesis, Department of Electronics and Computer Science, University of Southampton.

[138] K. Popper (1963), *Conjectures and Refutations*, Routledge.

[139] T.F. Quatieri and R.J. McAulay (1989), 'Phase coherence in speech reconstruction for enhancement and coding applications', *Proc. Int. Conf. Acoustics, Speech and Signal Processing*, 207-210.

[140] T.C. Rand (1974), 'Dichotic release from masking for speech', *J. Acoust. Soc. Am.*, **55**, 678-680.

[141] W.S. Rhode (1971), 'Observations of the vibration of the basilar membrane in squirrel monkeys using the Mossbauer technique', *J. Acoust. Soc. Am.*, **49**, 1218-1231.

[142] M.R. Riley (1989), *Speech Time-Frequency Representations*, Kluwer Academic Publishing.

[143] J.E. Rose, J.F. Brugge, D.J. Anderson and J.E. Hind (1967), 'Phase-locked response to low-frequency tones in single auditory nerve fibres in the squirrel monkey', *J. Neurophys.*, **30**, 769-793.

[144] S. Ross (1982), 'A model of the hair cell - primary fibre complex', *J. Acoust. Soc. Am.*, **71**, 926-941.

[145] I.J. Russell (1987), 'The physiology of the organ of Corti', *British Medical Bulletin*, **43**, 4, 802-820.

[146] M.B. Sachs and P.J. Abbas (1974), 'Rate versus level functions for auditory-nerve fibres in cats: Tone-burst stimuli', *J. Acoust. Soc. Am.*, **56**, 1835-1847.

[147] M.B. Sachs, H.F. Voigt and E.D. Young (1983), 'Auditory-nerve representation of vowels in background noise', J. Neurophysiol., **50**, 1, pp. 27-45.

[148] M.B. Sachs, C.C. Blackburn and E.D. Young (1988), 'Rate-place and temporal-place representations of vowels in the auditory nerve and anteroventral cochlear nucleus', *J. Phonetics*, **16**, 37-53.

[149] B. Scharf and C.H. Meiselman (1977), 'Critical bandwidth at high intensities', in: *Psychophysics and Physiology of Hearing*, E.F. Evans and J.P. Wilson (eds), Academic Press, New York, 221-232.

[150] M.T.M. Scheffers (1983), *Sifting Vowels: Auditory Pitch Analysis and Sound Segregation*, Ph.D. Thesis, Groningen University.

[151] D. Schofield (1985), 'Visualisations of speech based on a model of the peripheral auditory system', *UK National Physical Laboratory Report 62/85*, HMSO.

[152] M.R. Schroeder and J.L. Hall (1974), 'Model for mechanical to neural transduction in the auditory receptor', *J. Acoust. Soc. Am.*, **55**, 1055-1060.

[153] H.A. Schwid and C.D. Geisler (1982), 'Multiple reservoir model of neurotransmitter release by a cochlear inner hair cell', *J. Acoust. Soc. Am.*, **72**, 1435-1440.

[154] D.A. Seggie (1986), 'The application of the analytic signal analysis in speech', *Proc. Inst. of Acoustics*, **8**, 7,85-92.

[155] P.M. Sellick and I.J. Russell (1980), 'The responses of inner hair cells to basilar membrane velocity during low frequency auditory stimulation in the guinea pig cochlea', *Hearing Research*, **2**, 439-446.

[156] S. Seneff (1984), 'Pitch and spectral estimation of speech based on auditory synchrony model', *Proc. IEEE Int. Conf. Acoustics, Speech and Signal Processing*, San Diego, paper 36.2.

[157] S. Seneff (1986), 'A computational model for the peripheral auditory system: Application to speech recognition research', *Proc. IEEE Int. Conf. Acoustics, Speech and Signal Processing*, Toyko, 1983-1986.

[158] S. Seneff (1987), 'Vowel recognition based on line-formants derived from an auditory-based spectral representation', DARPA review meeting, San Diego.

[159] S. Seneff (1988), 'A joint synchrony/mean-rate model of auditory speech processing', *J. Phonetics*, **16**, 55-76.

[160] S.A. Shamma (1985), 'Speech processing in the auditory system I. Representation of speech sounds in the responses of the auditory nerve', *J. Acoust. Soc. Am.*, **78**, 1612-1621.

[161] S.A. Shamma, R.S. Chadwick, W.J. Wilbur, K.A. Morrish and J. Rinzel (1986), 'A biophysical model of cochlear processing: Intensity dependence of pure tone responses', *J. Acoust. Soc. Am.*, **80**, 133-145.

[162] S. Shamma (1988), 'The acoustic features of speech sounds in a model of auditory processing: vowels and voiceless fricatives', *J. Phonetics*, **16**, 77-91.

[163] W.P. Shofner and M.B. Sachs (1986), 'Representation of a low-frequency tone in the discharge rate of populations of auditory nerve fibres', *Hearing Research*, **21**, 91-95.

[164] D.G. Sinex and C.D. Geisler (1983), 'Responses of auditory-nerve fibres to consonant-vowel syllables', *J. Acoust. Soc. Am.*, **73**, 602-615.

[165] M. Slaney and R.F. Lyon (1990), 'A perceptual pitch detector', *Proc. IEEE Int. Conf. Acoustics, Speech and Signal Processing*, Alburquerque, 357-360.

[166] R.L. Smith and J.J. Zwislocki (1975), 'Short term adaptation and incremental responses in single auditory-nerve fibres', *Biol. Cybernet.*, **17**, 169-182.

[167] R.L. Smith and M.L. Brachman (1980), 'Dynamic responses of single auditory-nerve fibres: Some effects of intensity and time', in: *Psychophysical, Physiological and Behavioural Studies in Hearing*, G. van den Brink and A. Bilsen (eds), The Netherlands: Delft University Press.

[168] R.L. Smith and M.L. Brachman (1982), 'Adaptation in auditory-nerve fibres: A revised model', *Biol. Cybern.*, **44**, 107-120.

[169] R.L. Smith, R.D. Frisina and D.A. Goodman (1983), 'Intensity functions and dynamic responses fom the cochlea to the cochlear nucleus', in: *Hearing - Physiological Bases and Psychophysics*, R. Klinke and R. Hartmann (eds), Springer-Verlag.

[170] A.Q. Summerfield, A. Lea and D. Marshall (1990), 'Modelling auditory scene analysis: strategies for source segregation using autocorrelograms', *Proc. Inst. Acoustics*, **12**, 10 , 507-514.

[171] E. Terhardt (1987), 'The psychophysics of audio signal processing and the role of pitch in speech', in: *The Psychophysics of Speech Perception*, M.E.H. Schouten (ed), Martinus Nijhoff.

[172] H. Traunmuller (1987), 'Phase vowels', in: *The Psychophysics of Speech Perception*, M.E.H. Schouten (ed), Martinus Nijhoff.

[173] J.R. Trinder (1982), 'Hardware-software configuration for high performance digital filtering in real time', *IEEE Trans.*, 687-690.

[174] M.A. Viergever (1980), *Mechanics of the Inner Ear - A Mathematical Approach*, Delft: Delft University Press.

[175] C.S. Wallace and M.P. Georgeff (1983), 'A general objective for inductive inference', *Monash University Technical Report 32*, Department of Computer Science.

[176] M. Weintraub (1985), *A Theory and Computational Model of Auditory Monaural Sound Separation*, Ph.D. Thesis, Stanford University.

[177] M. Weintraub (1987), 'Sound separation and auditory perceptual organisation', in: *The Psychophysics of Speech Perception*, M.E.H. Schouten (ed), Martinus Nijhoff.

[178] T. F. Weiss (1966), 'A model of the peripheral auditory system', *Kybernetik*, **3**, 153-175.

[179] M. Wertheimer (1958), 'Principles of Perceptual Organisation', in: *Readings in Perception*, D.C. Beardslee and M. Wertheimer (eds), Van Nostrand, Princeton: NJ.

[180] L.A. Westerman and R.L. Smith (1984), 'Rapid and short term adaptation in auditory nerve responses', *Hearing Research*, **15**, 249-260.

[181] R.E. Wickesberg and C.D. Geisler (1985), 'Longitudinal stiffness coupling in a 1-D model of the peripheral ear', in: *Peripheral Auditory Mechanics*, S.T. Neely and A. Tubis (eds), 113-120, Springer-Verlag.

[182] S.M. Williams, P.D. Green and R.I. Nicolson (1990),'Streamer: mapping the auditory scene', *Proc. Inst. Acoustics*, **12**, 10, 567-575.

[183] R. Winslow (1985), *A Quantitative Analysis of Rate-Coding in the Auditory Nerve*, Ph.D. Thesis, John Hopkins University.

[184] A. P. Witkin and J. M. Tenenbaum (1983), 'On the role of structure in vision', in: *Human and Machine Vision*, J. Beck, B. Hope and A. Rosenfeld (eds), Academic Press.

[185] G.K. Yates, D. Robertson and B.M. Johnstone (1985), 'Very rapid adaptation in the guinea pig auditory nerve', *Hearing Research*, **17**, 1-12.

[186] G.K. Yates (1986), 'Reply to letter of Meddis', *Hearing Research*, **23**, 288-290.

[187] W.A. Yost and D.W. Nielsen (1977), *Fundamentals of Hearing - An Introduction*, New York: Holt, Rinehart and Winston.

[188] J. Zhao and P.N. Denbigh (1990), 'Pitch estimation for two overlapping voices', *Proc. Inst. Acoustics*, **12**, 10, 515-521.

[189] G. Zweig, R. Lipes and J.R. Pierce (1976), 'The cochlear compromise', *J. Acoust. Soc. Am.*, **59**, 975-982.

[190] J.J. Zwislocki (1973), 'On intensity characteristics of sensory receptors: A generalised function', *Kybernetik*, **12**, 169-183.

Index